HIKE
THE SAN GABRIEL
MOUNTAINS

Hike. Contemplate what makes you happy and what makes you happier still. Follow a trail or blaze a new one. **Hike.** Think about what you can do to expand your life and someone else's. **Hike.** Slow down. Gear up. **Hike.** Connect with friends. Re-connect with nature.

Hike. Shed stress. Feel blessed. **Hike** to remember. **Hike** to forget. **Hike** for recovery. **Hike** for discovery. **Hike.** Enjoy the beauty of providence. **Hike.** Share the way, The Hiker's Way, on the long and winding trail we call life.

HIKE
THE SAN GABRIEL
MOUNTAINS

BY
JOHN MCKINNEY

TheTrailmaster.com

HIKE the San Gabriel Mountains By John McKinney

Acknowledgments: For nearly 30 years of assistance in the field and from the office, a big thanks to the staff of Angeles National Forest. Thanks also for tips and trip details to Dan Simpson, avid San Gabriel Mountains hiker and blogger, and to Marianne and Gary Wallace, hikers with a deep appreciation and knowledge of the plants and wildlife found in these mountains.

ISBN: 978-0-934161-78-7
Book Design by Lisa DeSpain
Cartography by Tom Harrison (TomHarrisonMaps.com)
Cover photo by Tom Kenney
HIKE Series Editor: Cheri Rae

Published by Olympus Press and The Trailmaster, Inc. www. TheTrailmaster.com (Visit our site for a complete listing of all Trailmaster publications, products, and services.)

CONTENTS

San Gabriel River Area

High Country

Mt. Baldy Area

INTRODUCTION

Most of the San Gabriel Mountains lie just north of metro Los Angeles and within Angeles National Forest, one of the nation's most popular national forests for hiking. For more than a century the range has delighted Southland residents seeking quiet retreats and tranquil trails.

The San Gabriel Mountains are popular with hikers for good reason; in fact, for a lot of good reasons. An obvious reason for the range's popularity is its close proximity to the 16 million people living in the greater Los Angeles area. The region has a well-deserved auto-centric reputation, yet boasts one of the largest concentrations of hikers in North America. (Arrive early to find parking at such popular trailheads as Chantry Flat!)

The range's front country offers the hiker inviting arroyos, fine vista points and easy-to-access trailheads from the metropolitan flatlands. Angeles Crest Highway offers a scenic byway to the high country, grand mountain peaks and a wealth of taller trees.

My first hiking was in the San Gabriel Mountains with the Boy Scouts of Troop 441, Downey, California. When I was 12 years old, I hiked the 53-mile long Silver Moccasin Trail with a half-dozen boys and our Scoutmaster Arnold Blankenship.

I was the youngest and smallest of the group and still remember the butterflies in my stomach at the beginning of the trail at Chantry Flats Ranger Station. And then we were off—traversing up, down and through deep canyons and along the high ridges of the mountains. The landscape seemed to change every day, from lowland chaparral slopes to oak-lined canyons to fir and pine forests.

I still remember the intriguing names on the land: West Fork, Shortcut Canyon, Chilao Flat, Three Points, Cloudburst Summit, Islip Saddle...We put snow in our Sierra cups and stirred in Wyler's lemonade mix. No snow cone ever tasted so good. Little Johnny grew up a lot on that trip and, as the week progressed, I moved from the back of the pack to the middle to the front, until when it came time for summiting a couple of peaks, I passed everyone.

"Look out boys, Johnny has summit fever," our Scoutmaster declared, as I raced past the big guys. "Does that mean he has to go home?" one of the boys asked. "No, summit fever, that's a good thing," our leader explained. "You better catch it yourself or that little squirt is going to beat you to the top by half an hour."

Many years have passed since my scout days and yet I still get summit fever when approaching the San Gabriel Mountains. The mountains give me "Arroyo Fever" and "Foothill Fever," too. Surely a million more hikers have felt exactly the same way: hikers have been tramping the trails and enjoying the natural beauty of the mountains since the 1890s.

One of the first trail construction projects in the San Gabriels began in 1864 when Benjamin Wilson built a path to his timbering venture on the mountain that now bears his name. William Sturtevant, who came to California from Colorado in the early 1880s and became a premier packer and trail guide, linked and improved several trails and made it possible to cross the mountains from west to east.

More trails were built around the turn of the 20th century when Southern California's "Great Hiking Era" began. Many rustic trail resorts were later built to serve the needs of hikers. Today, only vintage photographs and scattered resort ruins remind us of these happy times, but that bygone era left us a superb network of trails—hundreds of miles of paths linking all major peaks, camps and streams.

I enjoyed sharing accounts of trails in the mountains during my long service as the Los Angeles Times Hiking Columnist. I—in fact, all hikers—owe a debt of gratitude to John Robinson, who described 100 hikes in *Trails of the Angeles*, first published in

1971 and still the best and most comprehensive guide to the trail network in Angeles National Forest. Robinson also wrote *The San Gabriels* and several excellent histories of the San Gabriel Mountains.

With a huge variation in terrain and elevation, the San Gabriel Mountains are not easily divided by geography into areas to hike. For purposes of geographic orientation, some recreation experts divide the San Gabriel Mountains into a front country and backcountry, foothills and high country. Sometimes the mountains are segmented into an east end, west end, south side, north side, city side, desert side, urban interface and alpine wilderness.

That's a bit too complicated for me. I focused on the task of selecting hikes you're sure to like in the foothills and front country, and from high country trailheads along Angeles Crest Highway.

HIKE the San Gabriel Mountains is an opinionated sampling of the range's delights, from the famed Arroyo Seco to foothills above the San Gabriel Valley to subalpine wilderness and tall summits. Some of the more challenging trails climb the towering backbone of the range, a 30-mile-long massif that includes the highest peaks in the range: Mt. Islip (8,250 feet) Mt. Baden-Powell (9,399 feet) and Mt. San Antonio (Baldy), the top summit at 10,068 feet.

Melting snow and rain flows from the shoulders of high peaks feed the range's largest river, the San

Gabriel. The river divides into a dramatic East Fork known for its fierce resistance to highway projects (and "Bridge to Nowhere") and a more mellow West Fork, renown for its trout fishing. Both forks, as well as famed Arroyo Seco, offer great hiking.

You'll find memorable day hikes along one of the nation's premiere long-distance trails, famed Pacific Crest Trail, which extends across the crest of the San Gabriel Mountains. And be sure to take a hike along another Trailmaster favorite—the 28.5-mile-long Gabrielino National Recreation Trail. The Forest Service, rarely given to bursts of lyricism, describes it thus: "This trail has been created for you—the city dweller—so that you might exchange, for a short time, the hectic scene of your urban life for the rugged beauty and freedom of adventure into the solitary wonderland of nature."

Let's start a second "Great Hiking Era" in the San Gabriel Mountains.

Hike smart, reconnect with nature and have a wonderful time on the trail.

Hike on,

John McKinney

Mt. Baldy: Awesome from any angle, including from the top of Strawberry Peak

EVERY TRAIL TELLS A STORY.

San Gabriel Mountains

Geography

Sixty miles long, 20 miles wide, the San Gabriels extend from Soledad Canyon on the west to Cajon Pass on the east. The mountains bless Los Angeles by keeping out hot desert winds, and curse it by keeping in the smog.

The San Gabriel Mountains, known as a Transverse Range, extend east-west across the state. The range is young (less than a million years in its present location), dynamic (it moves and grooves with the San Andreas Earthquake Fault), and complex; the fractured and shattered mountains are composed of many different kinds of rocks of diverse ages.

The San Gabriels are divided lengthwise into a steeper southern front range and a taller northern range by a series of east-west trending canyons. The southern foothills of the mountains rise abruptly 4,000 feet above the L.A. Basin. Mt. San Antonio (Baldy), at 10,068 feet the highest peak in the range, anchors the eastern end of the range.

Natural History

"The slopes are exceptionally steep and insecure to the foot and they are covered with thorny bushes from five to ten feet high" was how the great naturalist John Muir described the front range of the San Gabriels. The "thorny bushes" of Muir's description belong to the dominant plant community of the mountains—the chaparral.

Other front-range attractions are the arroyos. These boulder-strewn washes may seem dry and lifeless in the bottomland; however, a hiker following an arroyo's course upward may soon find lush creekside flora, including ferns and wildflowers, shaded by oak, sycamore and alder.

Higher elevations have a wealth of taller trees: Jeffrey pine, Ponderosa pine, lodgepole pine and the rare limber pine, as well as white fir and cedar.

A huge range of elevations (1,000 to 10,064 feet) means a diversity of environments and a wide variety of birds and wildlife. Larger mammals in the mountains include deer, bears, mountain lions, bobcats and the Nelson bighorn sheep.

History

First to use the mountains were the native Shoshone, or Gabrielino. For the most part they lived in the valleys and lowlands, and used the mountains for gathering food and hunting animals.

The Spanish gave the range two names: Sierra Madre (Mother Range) and Sierra de San Gabriel. Both were used until 1927 when the U.S. Board of Geographic Names decided upon the latter.

As early as the 1880s, it became obvious to Southern Californians the mountains should be protected from the destruction caused by indiscriminate logging and other ventures. In 1892, the San Gabriel Timberland Reserve was proclaimed by President Harrison. It was the first forest reserve in California, and the second in the U.S. (The first was Yellowstone.) The name was changed to San Gabriel National Forest in 1907, and to the Angeles National Forest a year later.

During "The Great Hiking Era," hikers rode Pacific Electric streetcars to trailheads in the foothills.

At the dawn of the 20th century, with President Theodore Roosevelt urging Americans to lead "the strenuous life," Southland hikers headed for the nearby San Gabriels and spawned "The Great Hiking Era." Soon every major canyon on the south side of the mountains had resorts or trail camps that offered hikers food and lodging.

Depression-era public works projects of the 1930s brought about a golden age of public campground construction. Angeles Crest Highway, built between 1929 and 1956, linked many of the best high mountain picnic and camping areas.

The 2009 Station Fire burned some 161,189 acres in the San Gabriel Mountains—including such iconic natural attractions as the Arroyo Seco and Mt. Wilson—and about 133 miles of trail. The fire burned for more than a month and by some accounts was the worst in Los Angeles County history, consuming 250 thousand acres and fully one quarter of Angeles National Forest.

Chaparral-cloaked slopes recovered quickly; pine-forested areas may take generations to re-grow. Credit volunteer trail-workers for a job well done; most of the trail system in the burn area has been restored and re-opened.

San Gabriel Mountains National Monument

In 2014, President Barack Obama designated 346,177 acres of U.S. Forest lands as the San Gabriel Mountains National Monument. The designation capped decades of efforts by conservationists to increase environmental protection for the San Gabriel Mountains, as well as to increase the recreation opportunities for the more than 4 million people per year who visit the Angeles National Forest.

In many ways it was easy to make the case that the mountains deserved an upgrade to national monument status. Two compelling reasons are its splendid natural beauty and its close proximity to the nation's second largest metropolitan area. Fifteen million people live within a 90-minute drive to the mountains.

The monument encompasses the northern and central regions of the San Gabriel Mountains and includes Mt. Baldy, Mt. Baden-Powell, and most major peaks. Sheep Mountain Wilderness, San Gabriel Wilderness and Pleasant Ridge Wilderness lie within the boundaries of the monument.

Thus far the monument is more symbolic than substance, since it lacks sufficient budget or a management team of its own. Unlike other national forests that face controversies and management issues over logging and energy development, the Angeles National Forest in general and San Gabriel Mountains

National Monument in particular must deal with the challenges of crowds. On a warm weekend, the shores along the East Fork of the San Gabriel River are as crowded as Southern California beaches.

Likely there will be more parking restrictions, traffic control, and fees implemented in years to come. For the hiker, though, national monument status for the San Gabriel Mountains is unlikely to change much of anything in terms of trails or the hiking experience. Hike on!

Adventure Pass

Many of the facilities and recreation areas in the Angeles National Forest/ San Gabriel Mountains National Monument are free, while others require an Adventure Pass or other fees. As a heads-up for hikers, more often than not in order to park at many of the trailheads, picnic grounds and other developed sites in the mountains, you need to purchase and display a Forest Adventure Pass. Cost is $5 per day, $30 annually.

The annual pass is also good for use elsewhere in Southern California in the Cleveland, San Bernardino and Los Padres National Forests. Learn more about the Adventure Pass, where its required, where to purchase one from the Angeles National Forest website.

My two cents worth of advice: consider purchasing a National Recreation Pass that's honored nationwide at Forest Service, National Park Service, Bureau of

Land Management, Bureau of Reclamation, and US Fish & Wildlife Service sites charging entrance or "amenity" fees.

Administration

The bulk of the San Gabriel Mountains (694,187 acres) is under the jurisdiction of Angeles National Forest, 701 N. Santa Anita Ave., Arcadia, CA 91006. Call 626-574-1613 or visit fs.usda.gov/angeles for the latest road and trail conditions, and information about user fees for campgrounds and select day-use areas.

For more information about Placerita Canyon County Park, call 661-661-7721 or visit placerita.org; for Eaton Canyon County Park, call 626-398-5420 or visit ecnca.org. Learn more about the good work of the San Gabriel Mountains Trail Builders at sgmtrailbuilders.org

*In many places in greater L.A., palms frame
vistas of the San Gabriel Mountains.*

EVERY TRAIL TELLS A STORY.

I
Foothills and Front Country

HIKE ON.

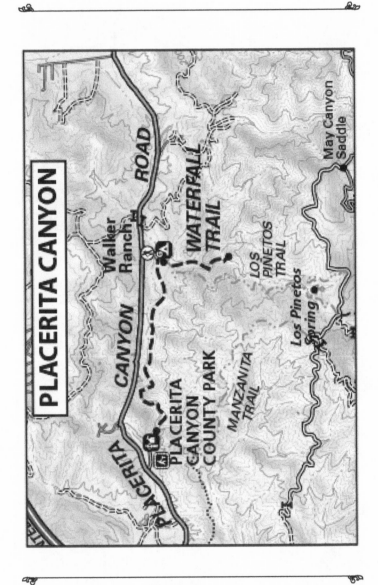

PLACERITA CANYON

PLACERITA CANYON ROAD

Walker Ranch

WATERFALL TRAIL

LOS PIÑETOS TRAIL

May Canyon Saddle

Los Piñetos Spring

MANZANITA TRAIL

PLACERITA CANYON COUNTY PARK

PLACERITA

TheTrailmaster.com

PLACERITA CANYON

CANYON, WATERFALL TRAILS

From Nature Center to Walker Ranch Picnic Area is 3.8 miles round trip with 250-foot elevation gain; to Los Pinetos Waterfall is 5.3 miles round trip with 500-foot gain

Placerita Canyon has a gentleness that is rare in the steep, severely faulted San Gabriel Mountains. A superb nature center, plus a walk through the oak- and sycamore-shaded canyon adds up to a nice outing for the whole family.

In 1842, seven years before the '49ers rushed to Sutter's Mill, California's first gold rush occurred in Placerita Canyon. Miners from all over California, the San Fernando Placers, as they became known, poured into canyon. The tree shading the spot where herdsman Francisco Lopez first discovered gold is now called the Oak of the Golden Dream.

Placerita Canyon has been the outdoor set for many movies, plus such 1950s TV westerns as "The

Cisco Kid" and "Hopalong Cassidy." Movie companies often used the cabin built in 1920 by Frank Walker. Walker, wife Hortense and 12 children raised cows and pigs, and panned for gold in the then remote canyon. Disney Studio's Golden Oak Ranch, located near the park, continues to make good use of Placerita Canyon as a movie location.

The recently upgraded Placerita Canyon Nature Center Museum excellent interpretive displays on native plants and wildlife. Highlights include a bird-viewing area with an observation deck and viewing scopes that allow visitors to watch wild birds and a wall-sized freshwater aquarium.

Short nature trails include Hillside Trail, which serves up views of Placerita Canyon, and Heritage Trail that leads to the Oak of the Golden Dream. My favorite is Ecology Trail (0.65 mile one way), which highlights a wide variety of native flora in the oak woodland, canyon bottom, and chaparral communities.

Canyon Trail meanders through Placerita Canyon to the park's group campground. From here, Waterfall Trail ascends along Los Pinetos Canyon's west wall, then drops into the canyon for an up-close look at the 25-foot fall.

DIRECTIONS: From Interstate 5 at Newhall Pass, take Highway 14 (Antelope Valley Freeway) 2.5 miles north and exit on Placerita Canyon Road. Turn right (east) and drive 1.5 miles to Placerita Canyon

County Park. Park in the large lot near the Nature Center.

THE HIKE: From the signed Main Trailhead, cross a bridge and follow Canyon Trail east up-canyon. Willows, alders, oaks and sycamores shade the creek banks.

The canyon narrows; it's gorge-like appearance is the result of thousands of years of natural erosion as well as a very destructive period of hydraulic mining in the 19th century.

About a mile out, the trail splits. The right branch stays on the brushy south side of the canyon while the left branch intersects a side trail ascending to a parking area on Placerita Canyon Road and then continues up-creek along the canyon bottom.

The two intersect a little short of the Walker Ranch Group Campground, where the hiker will find tables, water and restrooms.

Join Waterfall Trail (not to be confused with Los Pinetos Trail) and ascend into narrow Los Pinetos Canyon. Big-cone spruce, coastal live oak and a few stray big-leaf maples shade the canyon walls. The waterfall, sometimes an impressive flow after a good rain, splashes into a grotto at trail's end.

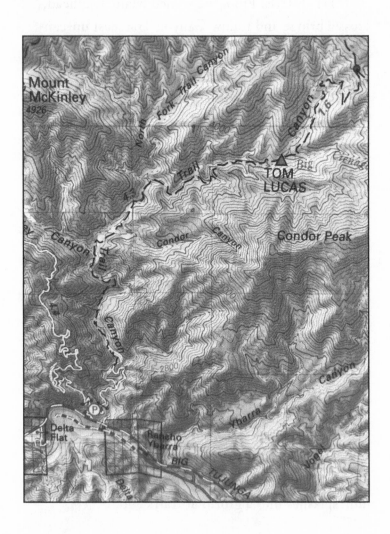

TRAIL CANYON

TRAIL CANYON TRAIL

To Trail Canyon Falls is 4 miles round trip with a 700-foot elevation gain

Trail Canyon Trail isn't quite as redundant as it sounds. The "Trail" in Trail Canyon refers not to a footpath but to the "trail" left by tiny flakes of gold found in the gravel of the canyon's creekbed. Turn of the century placer miners worked the creek, but the "trail" didn't lead to any riches.

The real wealth of Trail Canyon is in its scenery: steep canyon walls that conceal a bubbling creek and a surprising waterfall. The 30-foot waterfall is a classic beauty, framed by a steep-walled canyon, and with tall peaks in the distant background.

During dry months and drought years, the creek is a pokey watercourse, but swollen by rain and runoff it becomes lively, even raging. The path to the falls crosses the creek numerous times; be careful at times of high water.

While not exactly back to its former verdant splendor, Trail Canyon has recovered somewhat from the 2009 Station Fire that blackened this part of the forest. The west side of the range offers fewer trails than other parts of the San Gabriels, so hikers can give thanks to dedicated trail builders and be pleased that Trail Canyon Trail is open once more.

Beyond the falls, there's still work to be done, including clearing out the rugged route to 5,440-foot Condor Peak. This butt-kicker of a long all-day hike entailed ascending Trail Canyon Trail a long steep mile to a firebreak, climbing another long steep mile to a point just below the peak, then clambering over fractured granite to the summit. Reward for the dogged peak-bagger? Views of the San Fernando Valley, Santa Monica Bay and Catalina Island.

DIRECTIONS: From the Foothill Freeway (210) in Sunland, exit on Sunland Boulevard. Head east on Sunland, which soon merges with Foothill Boulevard. Continue a mile to Mt. Gleason Avenue, turn north (left) and drive 1.3 mile to its end at a "T" at Big Tujunga Canyon Road. Turn right, proceed 3.4 miles, and look carefully for dirt Trail Canyon Road on the left. Follow the road, which is suitable for passenger cars, (veering right at a fork) for 0.4 miles to a parking area. If you find a closed gate at the base of Trail Canyon Road, you'll need to hike 0.4 miles to the trailhead.

THE HIKE: The trail, a closed dirt fire road, passes private cabins (some in ruins, some occupied) that date from the 1920s and 1930s and arrives at the creek. The road ends and the footpath begins about 0.7 mile from the trailhead.

Cross and re-cross the creek a couple times as Trail Canyon Trail heads up-creek in the shade of sycamores, oak and alder. After another 0.6 mile or so, the path leaves the creek and switchbacks up the canyon's chaparral-covered west wall. After a couple of bends in the shade-less trail, as the canyon bends west, look for Trail Canyon Falls below.

At the 1.9-mile mark, you'll spot the side trail to the falls, a precipitous path, made by use, not design; proceed at your own risk. From the canyon floor, get an in-your-face view of Trail Canyon Falls spilling over a slick rock wall into a shallow pool.

To reach an observation point above the falls, continue another 0.1 mile. Keep hiking past this granite promontory and the trail soon descends to the creek again. You can follow use trails and rock-hop along the creek to the edge of the waterfall—an easier and safer option than the other very steep side trails. Enjoy the inspiring scene, but watch your footing and respect the considerable power of moving water.

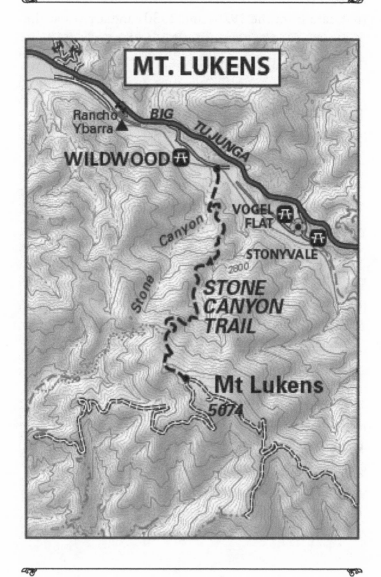

MT. LUKENS

STONE CANYON TRAIL

From Vogel Flats to Mt. Lukens is 8 miles round trip with 3,200-foot elevation gain

Mt. Lukens, a gray whale of a mountain beached on the eastern boundary of Los Angeles, is the highest peak within the city limits. A hike up this mile-high mountain offers a challenging workout and terrific clear-day views of the metropolis.

Theodore P. Lukens, for whom the mountain is named, was a Pasadena civic and business leader, and an early supporter of the first scientific reforestation effort in California. A self-taught botanist, Lukens believed that burnt-over mountainsides could be successfully replanted. During 1899 alone, Lukens and fellow mountaineers planted some 65,000 seeds in the mountains above Pasadena.

After the death of Lukens in 1918, a 5,074-foot peak was named to honor the one-time Angeles National Forest Supervisor and Southern California's

"Father of Forestry." Stone Canyon Trail is by far the nicest way to ascend Mt. Lukens. (Other routes are via long wearisome fire roads.) The trail climbs very steeply from Big Tujunga Canyon over the north slope of Lukens to the peak.

One warning: In order to reach the beginning of Stone Canyon Trail, you must cross the creek flowing through Big Tujunga Canyon. During times of high water, this creek crossing can be difficult and dangerous—even impossible. Use your very best judgment when approaching this creek.

DIRECTIONS: From Foothill Boulevard in Sunland, turn north on Mt. Gleason Avenue and drive 1.5 miles to Big Tujunga Canyon Road. Turn right and proceed 6 miles to Doske Road and make another right. Descend to Stonyvale Road, then left and drive 0.5 mile to a parking area at road's end.

THE HIKE: After carefully crossing the creek, begin the vigorous ascent, which first parallels Stone Canyon, then switchbacks to the east above it. Pausing now and then to catch your breath, enjoy the view of Big Tujunga Canyon.

The trail leads through chamise, ceanothus and high chaparral. Fires have scorched the slopes of Mt. Lukens. Stone Canyon Trail could use a few more shady conifers and a little less brush. Theodore Lukens and his band of tree planters would today be most welcome on the mountain's north slopes!

About 3.5 miles from the trailhead, intersect an old fire road and bear left toward the summit. Atop the peak is a forest of antennae. Old maps called the summit "Sister Elsie" before the peak was renamed for Lukens. As the story goes, Sister Elsie Peak honored a beloved Roman Catholic nun who was in charge of an orphanage for Native American children located in the La Crescenta area.

Enjoy the sweeping panorama of the Santa Monica and Verdugo mountains, Santa Monica Bay and the Palos Verdes Peninsula, and the huge city spreading from the San Gabriel Mountains to the sea.

Conservationist and civic leader Theodore Lukens (R) with his friend John Muir

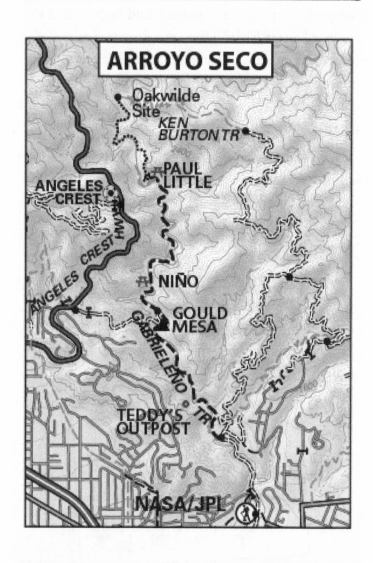

ARROYO SECO

- Oakwilde Site
- KEN BURTON TR
- PAUL LITTLE
- ANGELES CREST
- ANGELES CREST HWY
- NIÑO
- GOULD MESA
- GABRIELENO TR
- TEDDY'S OUTPOST
- NASA/JPL

Arroyo Seco

Gabrielino National Recreation Trail

From Windsor Avenue to Gould Mesa Trail Camp is 5 miles round trip with 300-foot elevation gain; to Oakwilde Trail Camp is 9 miles round trip with a 900-foot gain

During the early decades of the 20th century, Arroyo Seco was an extremely popular place for a weekend outing. About halfway up the trail stood Camp Oak Wilde, a rustic resort constructed in 1911. Hikers stayed a night or two or used the hostelry as a rest stop on the way up to Mt. Wilson. During the 1920s, a road was constructed and visitors drove the arroyo to Camp Oak Wilde.

Southern California's "flood of the century" wiped out Oak Wilde in 1938, along with the road leading to it. Ever since, hikers have walked the old 1920s auto road and newer Forest Service trails under a canopy of oak, sycamore, bay and alder to a trail camp and quiet picnic areas.

The path up the Arroyo Seco (part of the Gabriel-ino National Recreation Trail) is usually kept in good condition. However, the hillsides above the arroyo was badly burned in the 2009 Station Fire, a 10-mile length of the pathway was closed for many years, and it was not until 2018 that the whole trail re-opened.

Those who remember hiking the Arroyo Seco before the fire will notice a few changes. More stone steps, walls, foundations and other remains are visible now than in pre-fire days. And some of the bridges spanning the arroyo are closed or out of commission.

Arroyo Seco is the Southland's most storied canyon, with several inviting picnic areas located amidst the sylvan scene. This is a classic hike on a long popular path that connects the front range to backcountry and high country of the San Gabriel Mountains.

DIRECTIONS: From the Foothill Freeway (210) in Pasadena, take the Arroyo Boulevard/Windsor Avenue exit. Head north on Arroyo, which almost immediately becomes Windsor, and travel 0.75 mile. Just before Windsor's intersection with Ventura Street, turn into the small parking lot on your left. You can look down into the Arroyo Seco and see the Jet Propulsion Laboratory.

THE HIKE: Walk up Windsor to two roads. The leftward road descends to JPL. Head right on a narrow asphalt road (closed to vehicles), pass fenced-off areas and facilities belonging to the Pasadena Water

Department. After 0.5 mile, you'll hike past junctions with Altadena Crest Trail on your right and then a paved road on the left descending to Hahamongna Watershed Park.

Leaving the city behind, cross a bridge and continue north along the west side of the road. A mile from the trailhead, cross a second bridge and soon thereafter the road transitions to dirt and enters a sylvan scene, shaded by oaks and sycamores.

Continue up the arroyo on a wide path, crossing over a bridge back to the west side of the canyon, then back again on another bridge. Two miles from the trailhead you'll need to cross the creek on your own because the Elmer Smith Bridge is closed.

More creek crossings follow, you'll pass the foundation of an old bridge and the stone ruins of cabins, and arrive at Gould Mesa Trail Camp, which offers five sites.

From the camp, Gabrielino NRT continues ascending the arroyo, reaches Nino Picnic Area in 0.3 mile and then Paul Little Memorial Picnic Area with 0.7 mile more travel.

The arroyo twists and turns, climbs the east wall of the canyon to bypass Brown Canyon Debris Dam, then drops back into the arroyo and arrives at Oakwilde Trail Camp.

MILLARD FALLS

Millard Canyon is best known as the site of the Dawn Mine (see Dawn Mine hike), but it boasts a compelling natural attraction as well: 50-foot high Millard Falls. An easy half-mile path meanders along the floor of the narrow (less than 100 feet wide in places) canyon to the falls. This is a pleasant little hike, suitable for the whole family.

From the parking area, follow the dirt road through the tiny Millard Canyon Campground (5 tent sites). Locate the trail by the creek that flows across the dirt road. (If it's a strong flow, Millard Falls is likely to display a stellar cascade.) Depending on the water flow and your agility at rock-hopping, you might make it to the falls with dry feet. Or not.

Traveling under the shade of bay trees (sadly, many violated by carvings), the trail heads east along the narrow, woodsy canyon bottom. The path crosses the creek numerous times. About 100 yards from the falls, look left to spot steep Dawn Mine Trail, which makes a very steep ascent to get above the waterfall.

Millard Falls, hidden gem, and a great hike for kids

(A better route to the mine is via Sunset Ridge Trail. See description.)

From the base of the waterfall, enjoy the cascading beauty. (Don't try to climb up, over, or around the falls; people have been injured attempting this foolhardy ascent.)

DIRECTIONS: From the Foothill Freeway (210) in Pasadena, exit on Lake Avenue. Drive north 3.5 miles, at which point, Lake veers left and becomes Loma Alta Drive. Continue another mile to Chaney Trail Road and turn right. Follow the winding road for 1.5 mile as it ascends to Sunset Ridge, then down to the parking lot for Millard Campground and the trailhead for Millard Falls.

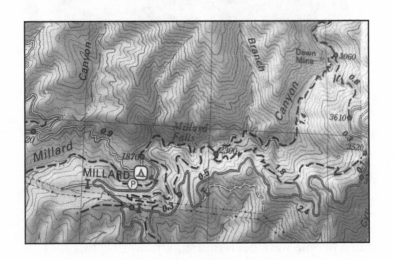

Dawn Mine

Sunset Ridge, Sunset, Dawn Mine Trails

From Sunset Ridge to Dawn Mine is 5 miles round trip with 1,400-foot elevation gain; optional return loop is 6 miles round trip

Hidden from the metropolis by Sunset Ridge, lush Millard Canyon is one of the more secluded spots in the front range of the San Gabriels. A cold stream tumbling over handsome boulders, a trail meandering beneath a canopy of alder, oak and sycamore, a waterfall and a historic mine, are among Millard's many attractions.

Millard Canyon is best-known as the site of the Dawn Mine which, unfortunately for its investors, produced more stories than gold. The mine was worked off and on from 1895, when gold was first discovered, until the 1950s. Enough gold was mined to keep ever-optimistic prospectors certain that they would soon strike a rich ore-bearing vein, but the big bonzana was never found.

Getting to the mine has for generations been a challenging hike—washed out trail, slow going with many stream crossings en route, piles of boulders and fallen trees. The Station Fire and the flooding and debris flow that occurred after the conflagration made Millard Canyon even more difficult to navigate. However, three cheers for the Restoration Legacy Crew that restored Dawn Mine Trail from beginning to end.

Even with easier going these days, the hike seems like an adventure—especially considering the trail's proximity to the metropolis.

DIRECTIONS: From the Foothill Freeway (210) in Pasadena, exit on Lake Avenue. Drive north 3.5 miles, at which point, Lake veers left and becomes Loma Alta Drive. Continue another mile to Chaney Trail Road and turn right. Follow the winding road for 1 mile as it ascends Sunset Ridge to a junction with Mt. Lowe Road and a turnout with a small trailhead parking area. If you can't find a space DON'T ignore the warning signs and park along the road; instead head 0.5 mile down to the parking lot for Millard Campground and the trailhead for Millard Falls at the end of the paved road.

THE HIKE: Walk up the Mt. Lowe Road, soon pass a junction with a trail leading down to Millard Campground, and proceed 0.3 mile to a junction with Sunset Ridge Trail. Go left on the footpath that travels to the canyon floor, just short of a mile from the trailhead.

Cross a bridge and the trail begins to dip in and out of the creek bed. If the creek is full, you'll notice inviting pools and swimming holes. Hike past check dams and, about 1.5 miles out, encounter evidence of the mining era: water pipes, wheels, cables suspended across the canyon.

The trail picks its way past cluster of boulders, bends west then north and *voila!*—the Dawn Mine.

I confess I was one of the many hikers from generations past who ventured into the mine—not a smart idea considering the darkness and deep holes filled with water. Well, those dangerous days are over: The mine entrance was closed and welded shut in 2017.

Return the same way or add a mile and loop back by picking up the trail across the canyon bottom from the mine, ascending a ridge, and switchbacking up to the right to continue the ascent to Dawn Station on the old Mt. Lowe Railway route at the 3-mile mark. Go south 0.2 mile, pass a junction with the Echo Mountain Trail, and soon meet and join the Sunset Ridge Trail.

The post fire-restored and reworked trail (good job volunteers!) makes for an enjoyable descent. Switchback along to Camp Sierra Picnic Area (4.2 miles out), rejoin Sunset Trail a mile farther, then return west the way you came back to the trailhead.

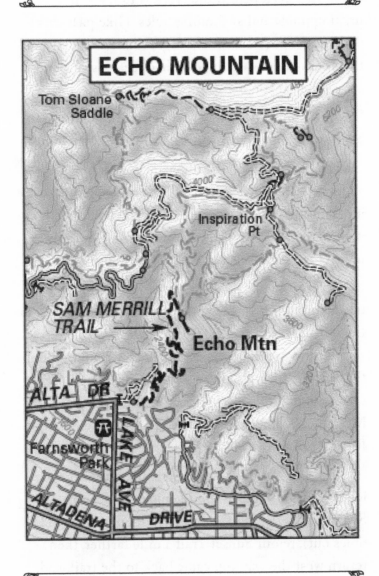

ECHO MOUNTAIN

Tom Sloane
Saddle

Inspiration
Pt

SAM MERRILL
TRAIL

Echo Mtn

ALTA DR

Farnsworth
Park

ALTADENA

LAKE AVE

DRIVE

TheTrailmaster.com

ECHO MOUNTAIN

SAM MERRILL TRAIL

From Cobb Estate to Echo Mountain is 5.6 miles round trip with 1,400-foot elevation gain

Professor Thaddeus Sobieski Coulincourt Lowe's Echo Mountain Resort area can be visited not only by retracing the tracks of his "Railway to the Clouds" (See Mt. Lowe Railway hike), but also by way of a fine urban edge trail that ascends from the outskirts of Altadena.

From Pasadena, visitors rode a trolley up Rubio Canyon, where a pavilion and hotel were located. Then they boarded the "airships" of the great cable incline, which carried them 3,000 feet (gaining 1,300 feet) straight up to the Echo Mountain Resort Area. "Breathtaking" and "hair-raising" were the most frequent descriptions of ride that thrilled tourists from the 1890s to the 1930s. Atop Echo Mountain was a hotel and observatory.

This historic hike visits the ruins of the one-time "White City" atop Echo Mountain. From the steps of the old Echo Mountain House are great clear-day views of the megalopolis.

Local citizens, under the auspices of the Forest Conservation Club, built a trail from the outskirts of Altadena to Echo Mountain during the 1930s. During the next decade, retired Los Angeles Superior Court clerk Samuel Merrill overhauled and maintained the path. When Merrill died in 1948, the trail was named for him.

Sam Merrill Trail begins at the former Cobb Estate, now a part of Angeles National Forest. A plaque placed by the Altadena Historical Society dedicates the estate ground as "a quiet place for people and wildlife forever."

DIRECTIONS: From the Foothill Freeway (210) in Pasadena, exit on Lake Avenue and travel north 3.5 miles to its end at Loma Alta Drive. Park along Lake Avenue.

THE HIKE: From the great iron gate of the old Cobb Estate, follow the trail along the chain-link fence. The path dips into Las Flores Canyon, crosses a seasonal creek in the canyon bottom, and begins to climb. With the earnest, but well-graded ascent, enjoy good vistas of the San Gabriel Valley and downtown Los Angeles.

After 2.6 miles of, steep and mostly shadeless travel, arrive at a signed junction with Mt. Lowe Railway Trail (see hike description). Bear right and walk 100 yards along the bed of the old Mt. Lowe Railway to the Echo Mountain ruins. Just before the ruins is a very welcome drinking fountain.

Up top, spot the railway's huge bull wheel, now embedded in cement, and just below a pile of concrete rubble, all that remains of the railway depot. The steps and foundation of the Echo Mountain House are great places to take a break and enjoy the view straight down precipitous Rubio Canyon, the route of Lowe's railway.

Echo Mountain takes its name from the echo that supposedly bounces around the semicircle of mountain walls. You can try shouting into the strategically placed "megaphone" to get an echo but perhaps even echoes fade with time.

Echo Mountain the easy way via the Great Cable Incline

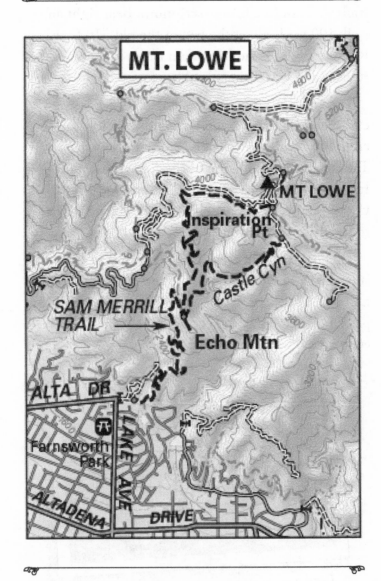

Mt. Lowe

Mt. Lowe Historic Railway Trail

To Echo Mountain, Mt. Lowe Trail Camp and Inspiration Point is 11-mile loop with 2,800-foot elevation gain

Professor Thaddeus Lowe, man of fame and fortune, was the quintessential California dreamer. His dream was to build a railway into—and a resort complex atop—the San Gabriel Mountains high above Pasadena. In the 1890s, his dream became a reality.

During the height of its popularity, millions took Professor Lowe's "Railway to the Clouds" to fine hotels and spectacular views of Southern California. Until it was abandoned in the 1930s, it was the Southland's most popular tourist attraction.

From Pasadena, visitors rode a trolley up Rubio Canyon, where a pavilion and hotel were located. Then they boarded the "airships" of the great cable incline, which carried them 3,000 feet (gaining 1,300 feet) straight up to the Echo Mountain Resort Area. From Echo Mountain, tourists could board a trolley and ride another few miles to Mt. Lowe Tavern at the end of the line.

Begin this journey back into history with a 2.6-mile hike to Echo Mountain (see hike description) to meet the Mt. Lowe Historic Railway Trail. The old railway bed has a gentle 7 percent grade for easy walking. You'll pass attractions that impressed an earlier generation of travelers: Granite Gate, Horseshoe Curve, and the site of the Great Circular Bridge. Ten stations mark the route and interpret the highlights.

DIRECTIONS: From the Foothill Freeway (210) in Pasadena, exit on Lake Avenue and travel north 3.5 miles to its end at Loma Alta Drive. Park along Lake Avenue.

THE HIKE: (See Echo Mountain hike description) After 2.6 miles of ascent, arrive at a signed junction with Mt. Lowe Railway Trail (Echo Mountain Trail). Begin the self-guiding interpretive hike over railroad ties still half-buried in the ground.

Here are the 10 stations along the railway trail with the hiking distances: Station 1 Echo Mountain; Station 2 View of Circular Bridge (0.5); Station 3 Cape of Good Hope (0.8); Station 4 Dawn Station/Devil's Slide (1.0); Station 5 Horseshoe Curve (1.2); Station 6 Circular Bridge (1.6); Station 7 Horseshoe Curve View (2.0); Station 8 Granite Gate (2.4); Station 9 Ye Alpine Tavern (3.4); Station 10 Inspiration Point (3.9).

Little remains at the site of Ye Alpine Tavern, but near this peaceful spot under oaks and big cone spruce is Mt. Lowe Trail Camp, with shade, water, restrooms and picnic tables.

From the camp, follow the fire road east and south for 0.5 mile to Inspiration Point, where there's a pavilion. Where the fire road makes a hairpin left to Mt. Wilson, go right. At Inspiration Point, gaze through several telescope-like sighting tubes aimed at Santa Monica, Hollywood, the Rose Bowl and more L.A.-area sights.

Return the way you came, but a faster way down is via Castle Canyon Trail, which begins below Inspiration Point and descends 2 miles to meet the railway trail just north of Echo Mountain. Hike Sam Merrill Trail back to the trailhead.

From Inspiration Point, take a look at metro L.A. and more through vintage sighting tubes.

RUBIO CANYON

Rubio Canyon offers a short hike into history and an up-close look at a double waterfall. The cascades—Moss Grotto Falls (the top one) and Ribbon Rock Falls (the bottom one)—have been a popular natural attraction for generations.

Beginning in the late 19th century, Pacific Electric Railway "Red Cars" delivered passengers from around the Southland to Rubio Canyon, where a pavilion and hotel were located. After taking refreshments, they boarded the "airships" of the great Mt. Lowe Cable Incline, which carried them 3,000 feet (gaining 1,300 feet) straight up to the Echo Mountain resort complex. In the early years of the railway, guests congregated at the stylish Rubio Pavilion, which was connected to the canyon by way of a system of wooden walkways and stair-steps. These boardwalk trails helped hikers easily reach the lovely waterfalls.

Nowadays to visit the falls, you need to take a hike from a nearby residential area. It's an easy jaunt, though. The hike along Rubio Canyon Trail to the falls is only 1.2 miles round trip with a 350-foot elevation gain.

Departing the Altadena residential area, the narrow footpath travels the brushy slopes on the western lip of Rubio Canyon. As you make a modest climb, you can look back and get vistas of the San Gabriel Valley and downtown L.A.

About 0.5 mile out, you'll spot bits of cement foundation where Rubio Pavillion once extended across the canyon. Just past the ruins, leave the trail and pick your way up-creek 0.1 mile to reach the double-tiered falls.

This is trail's end for most, though experienced hikers like to tackle Incline Trail (the old tram route) on the west side of the canyon up to Echo Mountain or to follow a sketchy trail up Rubio Canyon to Grand Chasm Falls.

DIRECTIONS: From the Foothill Freeway (210) in Pasadena, exit on Lake Avenue and head north 3 miles. Turn right on Dolores Drive, then in 0.4 mile make another right on Rubio Canyon Road. After 0.2 mile turn left to stick with Rubio Canyon Road, then turn right on Rubio Vista Drive and in another 0.2 mile locate the trailhead on the right between two houses.

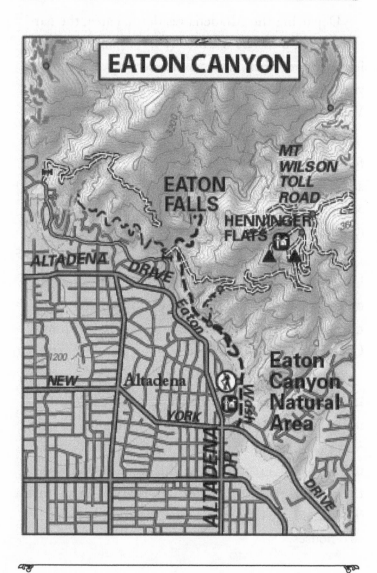

EATON CANYON

EATON
FALLS

MT
WILSON
TOLL
ROAD

HENNINGER
FLATS

ALTADENA DRIVE

Eaton

Eaton
Canyon
Natural
Area

NEW

Altadena

YORK

ALTADENA DR

WILSON

DRIVE

EATON CANYON

EATON CANYON TRAIL

From the Nature Center to Eaton Canyon Falls is 3 miles round trip with 200-foot elevation gain

Late one August afternoon in 1877, John Muir set out from Pasadena to begin his exploration of the San Gabriel Mountains. The great naturalist was very impressed with Eaton Falls, as he wrote in his book, *The Mountains of California*: "It is a charming little thing, with a low, sweet voice, singing like a bird, as it pours from a notch in a short ledge, some thirty-five or forty feet into a round mirror-pool."

Judge Benjamin Eaton channeled and piped the canyon's waters to nearby ranches. The judge's neighbors laughed when he planted grapevines, but the vines were quite profitable.

Much of the canyon named for Judge Eaton is now part of Eaton Canyon Natural Area. The park's nature center has exhibits that emphasize Southern California flora and fauna. Nature trails explore a variety of native plant communities—chaparral, coastal sage, and oak-sycamore woodland.

Eaton Canyon is a busy place on weekends. Family nature walks are conducted by docent naturalists; the park also has birdwalks, natural history classes and children's programs.

The walk up Eaton Canyon to the falls is an easy one, suitable for the whole family. Eaton Canyon Trail leads through a wide wash along the east side of the canyon to a junction with Mt. Wilson Toll Road; ambitious hikers can opt for a steep ascent of Mt. Wilson.

DIRECTIONS: From the Foothill Freeway (210) in Pasadena, exit on Altadena Drive. Proceed north 1.7 miles to the signed entrance of Eaton Canyon County Park. Turn right into the park and leave your car in the large lot near the nature center.

THE HIKE: From the parking lot, hike through the attractive grounds of the nature center. Cross the creek, then meander beneath the boughs of large oak trees and pass a junction with a connector trail that leads to the Mt. Wilson Toll Road.

The trail leads along the wide arroyo. Eaton Canyon has been widened considerably by repeated floods that have washed away canyon walls and spread alluvium, or water-transported sand and rock, across the canyon floor. It takes a hearty group of drought-resistant plants to survive in this soil. Notice the steepness of the canyon's walls. Early Spanish settlers called the canyon "El Precipio."

After a mile's travel from the nature center, reach the Mt. Wilson Toll Road bridge. A right turn on the toll road will take you on a long, steep ascent to the top of Mt. Wilson. A left turn on Mt. Wilson Toll Road leads a very short distance to the unsigned junction with Altadena Crest Trail. Walking 0.5 mile on Altadena Crest Trail to a vista point rewards the hiker with great clear-day views of the Los Angeles Basin.

To reach Eaton Canyon Falls, continue straight up Eaton Canyon wash. Rock-hop across the creek several times as you walk to trail's end at the falls. (Don't climb the falls; people have recently been injured and killed doing this.)

Eaton Canyon Falls: Easy to reach, easy on the eyes, extremely popular.

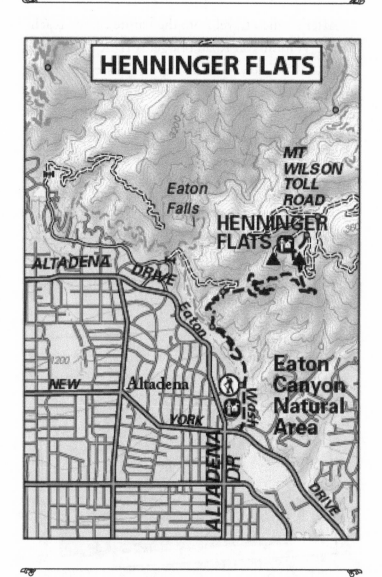

HENNINGER FLATS

Eaton
Falls

MT
WILSON
TOLL
ROAD

HENNINGER
FLATS

ALTADENA DRIVE

Eaton

NEW

Altadena

YORK

Eaton Wash

Eaton
Canyon
Natural
Area

ALTADENA DR

DRIVE

TheTrailmaster.com

Henninger Flats

Mt. Wilson Toll Road

From Altadena to Henninger Flats is 7 miles round trip with 1,400-foot elevation gain

Fortunately for California's cone-bearing tree population—and tree lovers—there is a place where trees, more than 120,000 a year, are grown to replace those lost to the capriciousness of nature and the carelessness of humans. The place is Henninger Flats, home of the Los Angeles County Experimental Nursery.

Perched halfway between Altadena and Mt. Wilson, Henninger Flats is the site of Southern California's finest tree plantation. On the flats you'll find reforestation exhibits and be able to view trees in all shapes and sizes, from seedlings to mature stands.

After careers as a gold miner, Indian fighter and first Sheriff of Santa Clara County, Captain William Henninger came to Los Angeles to retire in the early 1880s. While prospecting, Henninger discovered the little mesa that would soon bear his name.

Atop the flats he built a cabin, planted fruit trees, raised hay and corn. His solitude ended in 1890 when the Mt. Wilson Toll Road was constructed for the purpose of carrying the great telescope up to the new observatory. Henninger's Flats soon became a water and rest stop for hikers, riders and fishermen who trooped into the mountains.

After Henninger's death in 1895, the flats became a U.S. Forest Service tree nursery. Foresters emphasized the nurturing of fire- and drought-resistant varieties of conifers. Many thousands of seedlings were transplanted to fire- and flood-ravaged slopes all over the Southland. Since 1928, Los Angeles County foresters have continued the good work at Henninger Flats.

A moderate outing on good fire road, the trail to Henninger Flats is suitable for the whole family. The flats offer a large picnic area and fine city views.

DIRECTIONS: From the Foothill Freeway (210) in Pasadena, exit on Altadena Drive. Proceed north 1.7 miles to the signed entrance of Eaton Canyon Park. Turn right into the and park in the large lot near the nature center.

THE HIKE: Cross the creek and bear left, following the well-traveled path meandering beneath the boughs of large oak trees to a junction with the signed connector trail (often called the "equestrian trail") leading to Mt. Wilson Toll Road. Turn right and ascend this steep, long footpath to the toll road and turn right. The road begins a series of switchbacks up chaparral-covered slopes. Occasional painted pipes mark your progress.

Henninger Flats welcomes the hiker with water, shade, and two campgrounds. At the visitor center, view a huge pinecone display and learn about the natural and social history of the San Gabriel Mountans. The flats host some of Califonia's more common cone-bearing trees including knobcone, Coulter, sugar, gray and Jeffrey pine, as well as such exotics as Japanese black pine and Himalayan white pine.

After your tree tour, return the same way. Ultra-energetic hikers will continue up the old toll road to Mt. Wilson; the journey to the summit is 9 miles one-way with an elevation gain of 4,500 feet.

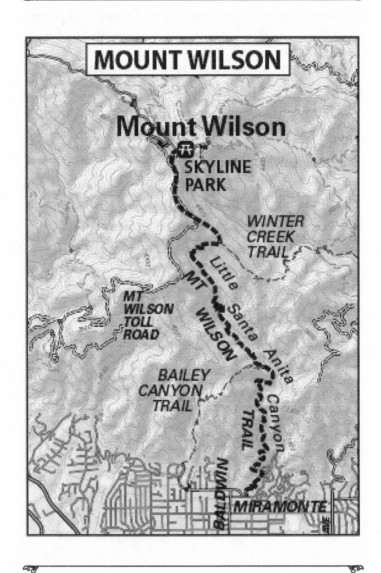

MOUNT WILSON

Mount Wilson

SKYLINE PARK

WINTER CREEK TRAIL

MT WILSON TOLL ROAD

Little Santa Anita

MT WILSON

Canyon TRAIL

BAILEY CANYON TRAIL

BALDWIN

MIRAMONTE

TheTrailmaster.com

MOUNT WILSON

MT. WILSON TRAIL

From Sierra Madre to Orchard Camp is 7 miles round trip with a 2,000-foot elevation gain; to Mt. Wilson is 15 miles round trip with a 4,500-foot gain

The tale of Mt. Wilson Trail begins with Benjamin Davis Wilson, who gazed up at the commanding peak located high above his San Gabriel Valley vineyard and figured those stands of pine and cedar on the mountain's shoulders would be an ideal source of timber. He built the first trail to "Wilson's Peak" in 1864.

The old trail was hugely popular when a hiking fervor known as the "Great Hiking Era" swept the Southland. In 1905 the Pacific Electric Railway extended its trolley service to Sierra Madre, reaching within 0.25 mile of the trailhead. Some 40,000 travelers passed through trail mid-point, Orchard Camp, in 1911.

Near the trailhead stands Lizzie's Trail Inn, built in 1895 and long known as an eatery for hikers. It's now a mountains history museum.

This hike leads up Little Santa Anita Canyon, visits Orchard Camp, and climbs to the top of Mt. Wilson, site of famed Mt. Wilson Observatory. It's a classic climb, and one of SoCal's nicest all-day hikes.

DIRECTIONS: From the Foothill Freeway (210) in Arcadia, exit on Baldwin Avenue and head north 1.5 miles. Turn right on East Miramonte Avenue and travel 0.2 mile near to Mt. Wilson Trail Road, which is on your left. Park on Miramonte or along Mt. Wilson Trail Road. The trail begins 150 yards up this road and is marked by a large wooden sign. After passing some homes, the trail shortly intersects the main trail.

THE HIKE: The path ascends the west side of Little Santa Anita Canyon. A mile from the trailhead, the path reaches a switchback that begins a half-mile section of pathway re-routed around a frequently washed out and eroded length of trail.

At 1.5 miles, the trail splits and an older branch descends to the bottom of the canyon to a locale named First Water. Stay left and take the trail into the increasingly narrow canyon.

The trail angles westward into Lost Canyon, crosses a creek and ascends past oak to a junction with a connector trail that ascends north to meet Bailey Canyon Trail. Soon thereafter, where Mt. Wilson Trail bends left, a path continues straight 100 feet to a clearing (helipad) that offers fine vistas.

At about the three-mile mark, the path descends to Decker Spring, returns to the main canyon, then continues another 0.5-mile to Orchard Camp, a shady glen dotted with oak and spruce trees. Homesteaders tried their hands at planting apple and cherry trees—hence the name Orchard Camp.

The trail continues through thick chaparral up Santa Anita Canyon to its head. It contours on the shelf-like trail, heads east on a firebreak, and crosses over a steep manzanita-covered ridge. At the intersection with Winter Creek Trail, turn left (west) and ascend steeply to Mt. Wilson Toll Road, 2 miles from Orchard Camp.

Turn right on the Toll Road and ascend a mile to Mt. Wilson Road, just outside Skyline Park.

What we've learned from Mt. Wilson Observatory: The universe is expanding and extends way beyond the Milky Way Galaxy.

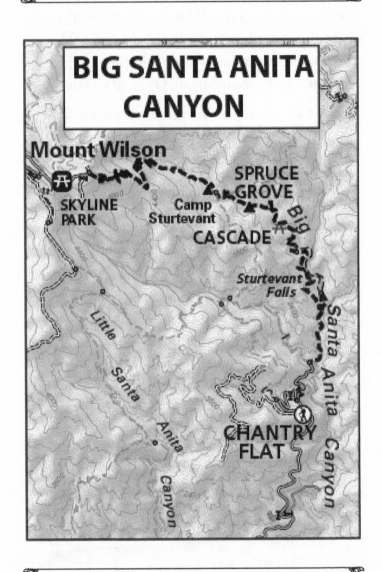

BIG SANTA ANITA
CANYON

Mount Wilson

SKYLINE PARK

Camp Sturtevant

SPRUCE GROVE

CASCADE

Sturtevant Falls

Little Santa Anita Canyon

Big Santa Anita Canyon

CHANTRY FLAT

TheTrailmaster.com

BIG SANTA ANITA CANYON

GABRIELINO NATIONAL
RECREATION TRAIL

From Chantry Flat to Sturtevant Falls is 3.5 miles round trip with 500-foot gain; to Spruce Grove Camp is 8 miles round trip with 1,400-foot gain; to Mt. Wilson is 8 miles one-way with 4,000-foot gain

Cascades, a waterfall and giant woodwardia ferns are a few of the many delights of historic Big Santa Anita Canyon. The bucolic canyon has been popular with hikers for more than a hundred years.

Burro-packer William Sturtevant pioneered many miles of San Gabriel Mountains trails.

"Sturde" hewed out a trail over the ridge from Winter Creek to the top of the canyon and in 1898 opened Sturtevant Camp; it was a popular trail resort well into the 1930s.

Sturtevant's trail is now a section of 28-mile long Gabrielino National Recreation Trail.

Hikers may continue past the falls to Spruce Grove Camp and to the top of Mt. Wilson.

DIRECTIONS: From the Foothill Freeway (210) in Arcadia, exit on Santa Anita Avenue and drive six miles north to its end at Chantry Flat. The trail begins across the road from the often jammed parking area. Arrive early or you might have to park way down the road and add miles or road-walking to your hike.

THE HIKE: Descend on the paved fire road, part of Gabrielino Trail, into Big Santa Anita Canyon. At the bottom of the canyon, cross a footbridge near the confluence of Big Santa Anita and Winter creeks. Here a small sign commemorates Roberts Camp, a resort camp founded in 1912.

Thanks to 1960s-era check-dams, the creek flows in well-organized fashion, lingering in tranquil pools, and then spilling over the dams in 15-foot cascades. Moss, ferns, alders and other creekside flora have softened the appearance of the dams and they now fit much better into the lovely surroundings.

The trail passes private cabins and reaches a three-way trail junction. To visit Sturtevant Falls, continue straight ahead. Cross Big Santa Anita Creek, then re-cross where the creek veers leftward. Pick your way along the boulder-strewn creek bank a final hundred yards to the falls. The falls drops in a silver stream 50 feet to a natural rock bowl.

Two signed trails lead toward Spruce Grove Trail Camp. The leftward one zigzags high up on the canyon wall; the other passes above the falls. The left trail is easier hiking while the right trail heads through the heart of the canyon and is prettier.

After a mile, the trails rejoin. Continue along the spruce-shaded path to Cascade Picnic Area. Call it a day here or ascend another mile to Spruce Grove Trail Camp. Both locales offer picnic tables and shade.

Hikers in top condition will charge up the trail to Mt. Wilson—an 8-mile (one way) journey from Chantry Flat. Continue on the trail up-canyon a short distance and cross the creek to a trail junction. A left brings you to historic Sturtevant Camp, now owned by the Methodist Church. The trail to Mt. Wilson soon departs Big Santa Anita Canyon and travels many a switchback through the thick forest to the summit.

Sturtevant, one of SoCal's most attractive waterfalls

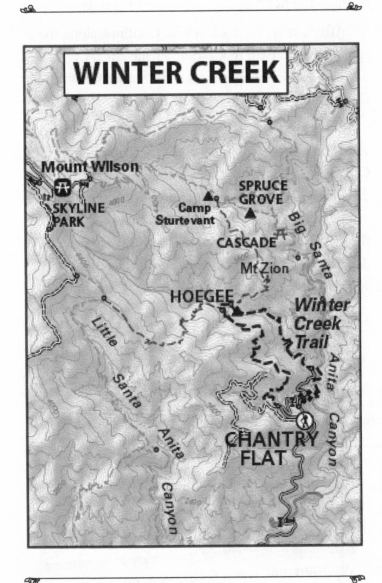

WINTER CREEK

Mount Wilson

SKYLINE PARK

SPRUCE GROVE

Camp Sturtevant

CASCADE

Mt Zion

Big Santa

HOEGEE

Winter Creek Trail

Little Santa

Anita Canyon

Anita Canyon

CHANTRY FLAT

TheTrailmaster.com

WINTER CREEK

WINTER CREEK TRAIL

From Chantry Flat to Hoegees Camp is 5.1 miles round trip with 1,000-foot total elevation gain; return via Mt. Zion Trail and Gabrielino Trails is 9 miles round trip with 1,500-foot gain

Before the dawn of the 20th century, packer/entrepreneur William Sturtevant set up a trail camp in one of the woodsy canyons on the south-facing slope of Mt. Wilson. This peaceful creekside refuge from city life was called Sturtevant's Winter Camp.

In later years the name Winter was given to the creek whose headwaters arise from the shoulder of Mt. Wilson and tumble southeasterly into Big Santa Anita Canyon. The hike along the creek is one of my favorites of the half-dozen that depart from the popular Chantry Flat Trailhead.

In 1908, Arie Hoegee and his family built a resort here that soon became a popular destination for Mt. Wilson-bound hikers; it remained so until battered by the great flood of 1938. A trail camp named for the Hoegees now stands on the site of the old resort.

DIRECTIONS: From the Foothill Freeway (210) in Arcadia, exit on Santa Anita Avenue and drive six miles north to its end at Chantry Flat. The trail begins across the road from the parking area. Arrive early or you might have to park way down the road and add miles of road-walking to your hike.

THE HIKE: Descend 0.75 mile on the paved fire road, part of signed Gabrielino Trail, into Big Santa Anita Canyon. At the bottom of the canyon, cross a footbridge near the confluence of Big Santa Anita and Winter Creeks.

After crossing the bridge, look leftward for the signed Lower Winter Creek Trail. Following the bubbling creek, the trail tunnels beneath the boughs of oak and alder, willow and bay.

Pass some cabins, built early in the 20th century and reached only by trail. The needs of the cabin owners have long been supplied by pack train. When you see man and beast moving through the forest, it's easy to imagine that you've stepped a century back in time, back into Southern California's Great Hiking and Trail Resort Era.

After crossing Winter Creek, arrive at Hoegees Camp. Tables beneath the big-cone spruce offer fine picnicking. Most signs of the original Hoegees Camp are gone, with the exception of flourishing patches of ivy. (In later years, Hoegees was renamed Camp Ivy.)

Walk through the campground until you spot a trail sign. Cross Winter Creek here and bear left on the trail. Soon you'll pass a junction with Mt. Zion Trail, a steep trail that climbs over the mountain to Sturtevant Camp and Big Santa Anita Canyon.

After re-crossing the creek, pass a junction with a trail leading to Mt. Wilson and join Upper Winter Creek Trail. This trail contours around a ridge onto open chaparral-covered slopes and offers fine clear-day views of Sierra Madre and Arcadia. The trail joins a fire road just above Chantry Flat and you follow this road through the picnic area back to the parking lot.

Generations of hikers have found peace and beauty in Big Santa Anita Canyon.

HERMIT FALLS

Hermit Falls, in contrast to nearby Sturtevant Falls, is relatively unknown and less visited, but nevertheless is one of the more popular hiking destinations in the San Gabriel Mountains. You could spend a wonderful day exploring Big Santa Canyon and visiting 30-foot Hermit Falls and 50-foot Sturtevant Falls.

On a warm day, expect plenty of company at Hermit Falls: hikers, swimmers, and, yes, cliff-jumpers. Hermit Falls is all over social media, and you're likely to observe jumpers recording their leaps to share on Instagram and everywhere else.

The hike to Hermit Falls via Gabrielino and First Water trails is 2.6 miles round trip with 650-foot elevation gain. This is an upside-down hike: you descend to the falls and hike uphill back to the trailhead.

I'm sad to report: taggers relentlessly desecrate the boulders around Hermit Falls with graffiti. Clean-up teams act quickly to erase it, but can't keep up with the vandalism.

To begin the hike to the falls, descend the paved fire road (part of the 28-mile long Gabrielino National Recreation Trail) 0.2 mile to the signed junction on the right with First Water Trail that leads to Hermit Falls. The path switchbacks down to the bottom of Big Santa Anita Canyon. About 0.75 mile from Chantry Flat, the path passes some cabins, and crosses the creek.

The path to Hermit Falls heads down-canyon. Saunter amidst tall trees, sword ferns and maidenhair ferns, up the east bank of the creek, then descend to the pools above Hermit Falls. Great swimming holes!

Near trail's end you'll notice several rugged routes leading to the pool at the base of the falls. Jumpers made these sketchy trails; use them at your own risk and peril.

DIRECTIONS: From the Foothill Freeway (210) in Arcadia, exit on Santa Anita Avenue and drive 6 miles north to its end at Chantry Flat, where there is an often extremely overcrowded parking lot. Nearby Adams' Pack Station offers limited parking ($10 last time I was there). Arrive early or you might have to park way down the road and add miles of road-walking to your hike.

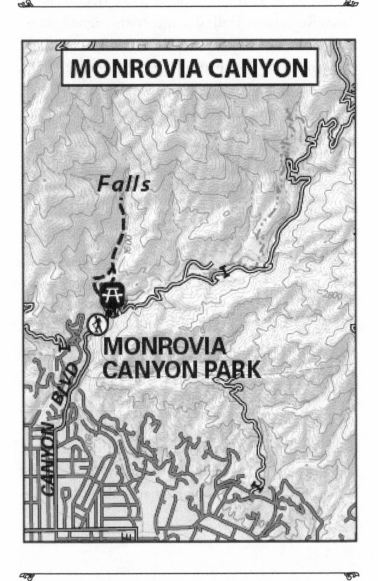

MONROVIA CANYON

Falls

MONROVIA CANYON PARK

CANYON BLVD

Monrovia Canyon

Waterfall Trail

1.5 miles round trip with 200-foot elevation gain

Shaded by live oak and sycamore, Monrovia Canyon Park is a delightful retreat with a little waterfall, nature trail and nature museum. A two-tiered waterfall cascades into an oak- and spruce-shaded grotto in the midst of Monrovia Canyon.

DIRECTIONS: From Foothill Freeway (210) in Monrovia, exit on Myrtle Avenue and go 2 miles north. Turn right on Scenic Drive, sticking with it as it becomes Canyon Boulevard and continues another mile to Monrovia Canyon Park (open daily except Tuesday, parking fee). Waterfall Trail begins opposite the picnic area near the nature museum.

THE HIKE: Descend to the canyon bottom to meet the park's nature trail heading down-canyon. Head up-canyon on the shady, creekside path past a series of check-dams to the base of the falls. Retrace your steps then extend the hike with the nature trail.

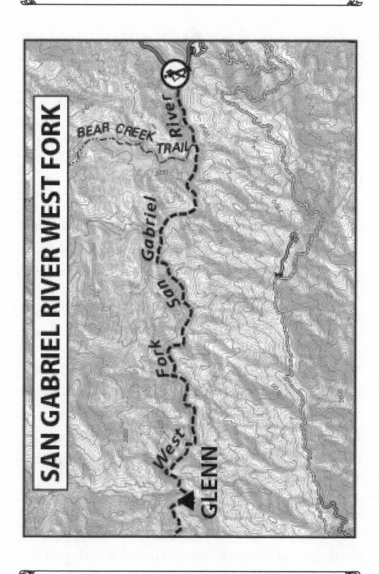

SAN GABRIEL RIVER WEST FORK

BEAR CREEK TRAIL

San Gabriel River

West Fork San Gabriel

GLENN

SAN GABRIEL RIVER
WEST FORK

WEST FORK NATIONAL SCENIC TRAIL

From Highway 39 to Glenn Camp is 14 miles round trip, but (much) shorter trips are possible

The San Gabriel River has two major forks, each with a claim to fame. East Fork is known for its gold, West Fork for its trout.

Early West Fork fishing camps catered to men looking for camaraderie, rustic accommodations and good fishing. The 1890s were a particularly grand time to cast a line. While most anglers caught no more than the limit—50(!) fish—others were greedy and some even used dynamite to "fish" for trout. California Governor Henry H. Markham was hardly an example of the conservation-minded sportsman; he landed 98 fish in six hours of fishing the West Fork.

Finally, the California Department of Fish and Game stepped in to enforce limits and replenish the

West Fork with fingerlings and trout brought in from Lake Tahoe.

West Fork is even today one of the Southland's best fishing rivers. Most of the West Fork has been set aside as a wild trout preserve. Fishing is of the "catch and release" variety. Barbless hooks must be used and the daily limit is zero. Fishing for keeps is permitted along a portion of the West Fork—a 1.5-mile length near the trailhead.

The river can be reached from a couple different directions, but most anglers, as well as hikers and bicyclists, join the West Fork Scenic Trail which departs from Highway 39. The trail, actually an asphalt road, meanders 7 miles with the river to shady Glenn Camp. (The road continues another 1.5 miles past Glenn Camp to Cogswell Reservoir, which is closed to the public, and connects with forest service fire roads heading west.) Walk the whole way to Glenn Camp or pick a picnic or fishing spot anywhere you choose.

DIRECTIONS: From the Foothill Freeway (210) in Azusa, exit on Azusa Avenue (Highway 39) and head north. Fourteen miles later, and 0.5 mile past the Forest Service's San Gabriel Canyon Off-Highway Vehicle Area and Rincon Fire Station, look for a parking lot and locked gate on your left. Signed West Fork National Scenic Trail is the asphalt road descending into the canyon.

THE HIKE: Head past the locked gate and down the road into the canyon. On the weekends, expect plenty of company along the first mile of trail. Many canyon visitors will be toting coolers, lawn chairs and fishing poles.

After a mile, intersect Bear Creek Trail that leads north into the San Gabriel Wilderness. Pioneers had many an encounter with a grizzly along this creek, which is how this tributary of the San Gabriel River got its name. After another 0.5 mile of travel, re-cross the river and enter the designated wild trout preserve.

The road, which climbs very slowly, but steadily, upriver leads past many, tranquil, oak- and sycamore-shaded pools. Seven miles from the trailhead reach Glenn Camp, set on a shady flat right by the river. It's a peaceful place with tables that invite a picnic.

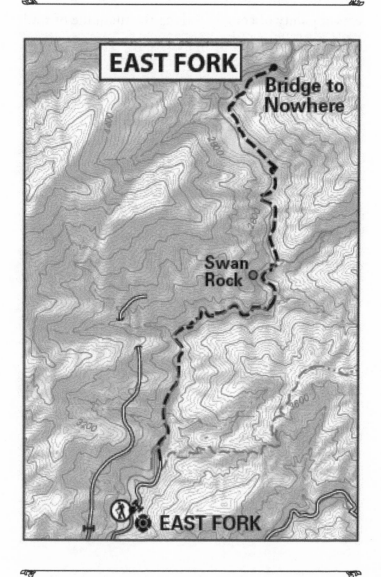

EAST FORK

Bridge to Nowhere

Swan Rock

EAST FORK

SAN GABRIEL RIVER EAST FORK

EAST FORK TRAIL

From East Fork Station to the "Bridge to Nowhere" is 9 miles round trip with 1,000-foot elevation gain

Sometimes a weekend gold miner finds a flash in the pan, but the real treasure of this section of the San Gabriel River lies in its beauty, its alders and tumbling waters. It's wet going; expect do a lot of wading, boulder-hopping and stream-crossing.

This hike leads through the monumental middle section of the East Fork of the San Gabriel River, and into Sheep Mountain Wilderness. The dizzy chasm of the Narrows is awesome, the steepest river gorge in Southern California.

Road builders of the 1930s envisioned a highway through the East Fork to connect the San Gabriel Valley with Wrightwood and the desert beyond. The great flood of 1938 interrupted these plans, leaving a handsome highway bridge stranded far up-river, the so-called "Bridge to Nowhere."

You'll pass the cracked asphalt remains of the old East Fork Road and gain access to the well-named Narrows, where the river flows 6,000 feet below nearby Iron Mountain.

The lower portion of the river is one of the most heavily visited recreation sites in the mountains, attracting crowds in the summer that rival those on crowded beaches. Expect access points to change as the recreation site goes through a major redesign and upgrade.

DIRECTIONS: From the San Bernardino Freeway (10) exit on Azusa Avenue (Highway 39) and head north. Ten miles up Highway 39, turn right (east) on East Fork Road and continue eight more miles to the East Fork Ranger Station. Park in the lot below the station.

THE HIKE: Follow the service road above the east side of the river 0.5 mile. Next, descend to the canyon floor and begin crossing and re-crossing the river. A bit more than two miles from the trailhead is Swan Rock, a mighty wall west of the river with the faint outline of a gargantuan swan.

As the canyon floor widens and twists northward, you'll climb up the right side of the canyon and continue up-river on the remains of East Fork Road, high above the rushing water. After ascending north a ways, you'll reach the "Bridge to Nowhere." No road meets this bridge at either end; the highway washed away in the flood of 1938. Bungee-jumpers love to leap from the bridge.

Cross the bridge and join a slim trail that soon drops you into The Narrows. A quarter-mile from the bridge, Narrows Trail Camp (just a wide spot on the bank) is a fine place to picnic and view the handsome gorge.

Hardy hikers will boulder-hop along between towering granite walls. Iron Fork joins the river from the left, six miles from the trailhead.

Up-river another mile from Iron Fork is Fish Fork, whose waters cascade from the shoulders of Mt. Baldy. It, too, has been a popular fishing spot for generations of anglers. You can slosh up Fish Fork for another mile before a falls and the sheer canyon walls halt your progress.

It became the "Bridge to Nowhere" after a 1938 flood wiped out the highway then under construction.

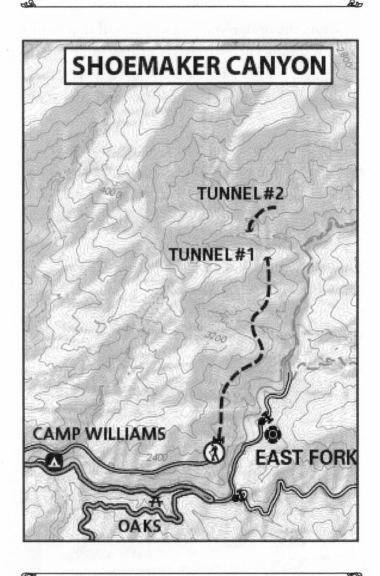

SHOEMAKER CANYON

TUNNEL #2

TUNNEL #1

CAMP WILLIAMS

EAST FORK

OAKS

TheTrailmaster.com

SHOEMAKER CANYON

SHOEMAKER CANYON TRAIL

From Shoemaker Canyon Road to Second Tunnel is 5.5 miles round trip with 800-foot elevation gain

With its towering rock walls and dramatic V-shaped gorge, the East Fork of the San Gabriel River is monumental in scale, boasting some of the most rugged relief in all of Southern California.

You'd think such forbidding terrain would discourage engineers from even thinking about building a highway up the East Fork to connect with Angeles Crest Highway. But no, two generations of roadbuilders have attempted to bulldoze, blast and bridge a road up the East Fork.

The first attempt began in 1929 when road crews constructed a highway in the lower reaches of the canyon. The "storm of the century" (March 1, 1938) hit the mountains and the swollen San Gabriel River ripped the roadway to pieces.

In 1954, engineers attacked the East Fork again. The Los Angeles County Road Department, using inmate labor, began constructing the highway high on the west wall of the canyon in order to avoid the possibility of another flood. Despite 15 years of hard work, only 4.5 miles of road were completed.

In 1969, county budget cuts and protests by conservationists led officials to halt highway construction. When the area gained wilderness status in 1984, there was little possibility the highway project would ever be revived. "Convict Road," as it was known back then, stands today as a monument to bad planning. Visitors may drive the first one-third of the road and hike the balance of the "Road to Nowhere." Hike highlights include two very long tunnels of early 1960s vintage and grand vistas of the East Fork of the San Gabriel River.

DIRECTIONS: From the Foothill Freeway (210) in Azusa, take the Azusa Avenue–Highway 39 exit and head north about 11.5 miles to East Fork Road. Turn right (east) and drive 3.3 miles to a junction with signed Shoemaker Canyon Road. Bear left and follow it 2 miles to the end of the paved road, a vehicle gate and a parking area.

THE HIKE: Step around the vehicle gate and begin a moderate ascent on the graded dirt road. Shade en route is scarce—limited to the towering walls left behind by the road cuts.

About 1.75 miles of hiking brings you to the first tunnel, an ambitious enterprise more than 1,000 feet long. The road narrows a bit, dips and climbs to a second tunnel, some 700 feet long.

Beyond the second tunnel, a brush-overgrown footpath continues 75 yards to the head of a steep ravine. It would not be a prudent move to cross over to a remaining length of road on the other side of the canyon.

To take in the sights—and sounds—of the mighty East Fork of the San Gabriel River, backtrack 75 yards or so on a brushy path leading south outside the tunnel. Admire the view of the grand chasm as well as mighty Iron Mountain in the midst of the Sheep Mountain Wilderness, and retrace your steps through the tunnels back to the trailhead.

Hike the high country! Hit the trail to Mt. Waterman and other tall peaks from trailheads along Angeles Crest Highway.

EVERY TRAIL TELLS A STORY.

II

HIGH COUNTRY

HIKE ON.

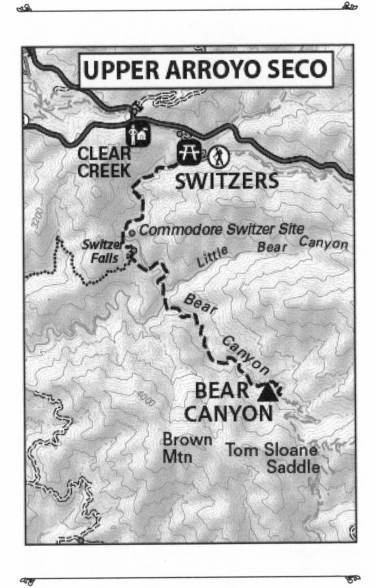

UPPER ARROYO SECO

CLEAR CREEK

SWITZERS

Commodore Switzer Site

Switzer Falls

Little Bear Canyon

Bear Canyon

BEAR CANYON

Brown Mtn

Tom Sloane Saddle

TheTrailmaster.com

UPPER ARROYO SECO

GABRIELINO NATIONAL RECREATION TRAIL

From Switzer Picnic Area to Switzer Falls is 4 miles round trip with 600- foot elevation loss; to Bear Canyon is 8 miles round trip with 1,000-foot gain

This classic walk through the wildest part of Arroyo Seco visits Switzer Falls and a trio of peaceful trail camps. A quiet stream—lined with colonnades of alder, live oak and mountain lilac clinging to the narrow sides of the gorge—cascades over boulders of big gray granite.

Perry Switzer, a carpenter who regained his health in the invigorating San Gabriels, built a trail up the Arroyo Seco and what became the most popular trail resort in the San Gabriels. Later owner Lloyd Austin added a tennis court, chapel, dance floor and a sign: "Leave your cares and animals this side of the stream." Switzer-land was popular with hikers well into the 1930s.

During The Great Hiking Era, a hiker could venture along the Arroyo Seco and within a half hour lose all signs of civilization. Amazingly, you still can today.

Note: Gabrielino Trail in its upper reaches to Oakwilde was wiped out in the Station Fire. Bear Canyon and Trail Camp are back in service if a bit worse for wear.

DIRECTIONS: Take Angeles Crest Highway (2) north from La Canada for 10 miles. A short distance past the junction of Angeles Crest and Angeles Forest (N3) Highways, note the Clear Creek Information Station on your right and continue 0.5 mile to parking on the right side of the highway. Walk down the paved road 0.25 mile to Switzer Picnic Area and the beginning of the trail at the lower end of the picnic grounds.

THE HIKE: Cross the bridge and follow the trail into the canyon. The pathway meanders with the stream under oak, alder and spruce. Cross and recross the stream several times.

In a mile, reach Commodore Switzer Site, perched on a bench just above the falls. The creek trail below the former camp dead-ends above the falls.

Cross the stream and follow the trail on the west slope, get a nice view of the falls and reach a signed junction. To the right (southwest) is the main trail down to Oakwilde and Pasadena. Bear left here and hike down into the gorge of the Arroyo Seco below the falls. When you reach the creek, turn upstream 0.25 mile to the falls. Heed the warning signs and don't try to climb the falls. Retrace your steps back to the trail junction.

To Bear Canyon Trail Camp: Continue down the Arroyo gorge. After 0.75 mile, the trail reaches Bear Canyon and heads east up the canyon, crossing and re-crossing the creek, passing many nice pools. The trail closely parallels the creek. Continue to Bear Canyon Camp, 2 miles up the canyon.

To Oakwilde: From the junction above Switzer Trail Camp, continue right on the Gabrielino NRT. The trail leaves the main Arroyo Seco canyon, crosses a chaparral ridge, and drops into Long Canyon. It then descends to Arroyo Seco creek bottom and follows the creek a mile to Oakwilde Trail Camp.

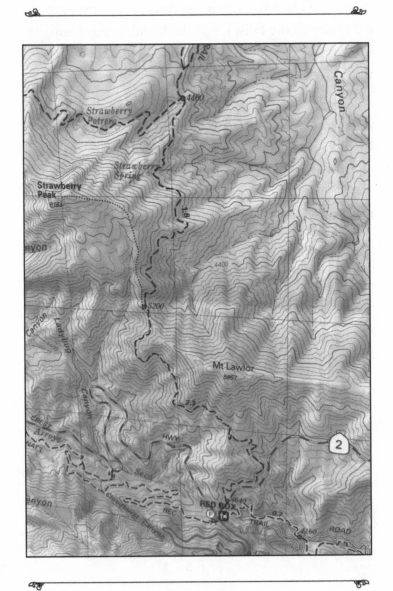

STRAWBERRY PEAK

STRAWBERRY PEAK TRAIL

**To Strawberry Peak summit is 7.5 miles round trip with
1,500-foot elevation gain**

Named by mountaineers of a century ago, who
imagined an upside-down strawberry, Strawberry Peak
offers a challenge to hikers wishing to climb it and
partake of the great views from its summit. The challenge comes from the final approach to the peak, which
involves scrambling over boulders and ascending a steep
ridge, gaining 950 feet of elevation in just 1.25 miles!

At 6,164 feet, Strawberry Peak just tops its
neighbor across the Angeles Crest Highway, San
Gabriel Peak (6,161 feet), for the honor of being the
highest peak in the front range of the San Gabriel
Mountains. Compared to the sometimes smoggy air
clinging to other city-facing front range peaks, the
air around Strawberry Peak is positively alpine.

Strawberry Peak always seems to me much more of
a backcountry peak than a front range one.

Yes, you eventually get metropolitan views from the summit, but the more memorable panoramas are those of the Arroyo Seco and Big Tujunga watersheds, and of the crests along Angeles Crest Highway.

I'm fond of the hike up Strawberry Peak because reaching the top requires more than the usual "walk-up" common to most summits in the range. No technical climbing skill or tricky navigation is involved, though. Just some dogged determination to make the summit.

DIRECTIONS: From the Foothill Freeway (210) in La Canada, drive 14 miles on Angeles Crest Highway (2) to Mt. Wilson Red Box Rd. At the turnoff is a picnic area and parking lot; park at the easternmost (farthest) end of the lot. Carefully cross Angeles Crest Highway and locate the start of the trail near road marker 38.42.

THE HIKE: Leaving power lines and the highway behind, the trail climbs brushy slopes. After an aggressive gain, the trail levels a bit as it contours around Strawberry's neighbor, Mt. Lawlor, and serves up views of Mt. Wilson and its observation domes.

About 2 miles along, you'll get your first views of Strawberry Peak. Descend the trail to Lawlor Saddle, a distinct gap between Lawlor and Strawberry peaks located 2.5 miles from the trailhead. From the saddle, Strawberry Peak continues 2 miles north to reach a junction with Colby Canyon Trail and Strawberry Meadow.

For peak-bound hikers, it's time to say goodbye to the official Forest Service trail and start trekking up the ridge to Strawberry Peak. Climb on. Alas, the route is not all uphill; it roller-coasters down in several places and the hiker must give up hard-won elevation and gain it back again. Measure your progress by looking back down at Lawlor Saddle. It is getting smaller, receding into the distance. Really.

The route splits into multiple narrow paths, but fear not. Just keep your eyes on the prize and keep hiking up the ridge. The summit is mostly brush covered (most of the Coulter pines were casualties of the 2009 Station Fire).

Particularly striking are views east of Mt. Baldy, high point of the range, and west to Mt. Lukens. On a clear day, get vistas of downtown L.A. and across the basin to the coast and Pacific Ocean.

Strawberry Peak, a favorite of hikers since the 19th century.

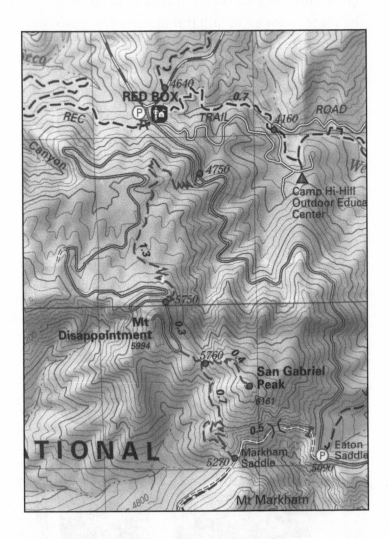

SAN GABRIEL PEAK

SAN GABRIEL PEAK TRAIL

To San Gabriel Peak is 4 miles round trip with 1,300-foot elevation gain; to Mt. Disappointment is 4.5 miles round trip

A splendid high view of mountain summits and the wide L.A. Basin is a hiker's reward for completing the climb to the top of the San Gabriel Mountains' namesake peak. Pyramid-shaped San Gabriel Peak, located at the crest of the front range, high above Altadena, offers a 360-degree view of basin and range.

From atop 6,161-foot San Gabriel Peak, you'll have the opportunity to look down on two of the Southland's most famous peaks: Mt. Lowe (5,603 feet) and Mt. Wilson (5,710 feet). Foothill Freeway commuters and other city-dwellers accustomed to looking up at these L.A. landmarks might enjoy seeing the two mountains from a different perspective and in a different light.

Well-engineered San Gabriel Peak Trail, built by the JPL Hiking Club in 1988, takes you to the top.

It's a no-nonsense ascent, beginning with aggressive switchbacks.

The trail to San Gabriel Peak also offers the hiker a chance to easily conquer a second summit—Mt. Disappointment.

In 1873, a survey party bushwhacked through the chaparral, attempting to locate the area's highest peak in order to establish a triangulation point for future mapmaking efforts. When the surveyors reached the summit of what they adjudged to be the highest peak, they were mighty disappointed to realize that another peak—nearby San Gabriel Peak—was 100 feet higher. "Mt. Disappointment" the surveyors named San Gabriel's sister peak.

Compared to lovely San Gabriel Peak, Mt. Disappointment is a homely summit. Back in the 1950s, the U.S. Army dynamited then flattened the summit, built a Nike missile site, and bulldozed a road. Today the peak is forested with communications antennae. Nevertheless, it's well worth your time to climb both peaks because they are so close together and because they offer differing vistas.

DIRECTIONS: From the Foothill Freeway (210) in La Canada, exit on Angeles Crest Highway (2) and drive 14 miles into the mountains to Red Box Station. Turn right on Mt. Wilson Road, proceed 0.3 mile, then make a right on the Mt. Disappointment service road, which leads to a small parking lot.

THE HIKE: The path switchbacks southeast up the pine- and oak-forested slopes. Occasionally paralleling the Mt. Disappointment service road, the trail offers eastward views of Mt. Wilson.

Nearing the top, the trail reaches, then joins the paved road. Climb a short 0.25 mile with the road to a junction. The road turns sharply right (almost a U-turn) and continues another 0.25 mile to the summit of Mt. Disappointment.

From the junction, bear left and join the unsigned footpath leading to San Gabriel Peak. The trail dips and quickly comes to an unsigned junction. The right fork descends to Markham Saddle and eventually links up with the Mt. Lowe trail system. Continue on the left fork, climbing southeast, first along the saddle between Mt. Disappointment and San Gabriel Peak, then up San Gabriel Peak itself. A stiff 0.5-mile climb takes you to the summit.

From here to infinity: the view from San Gabriel Peak.

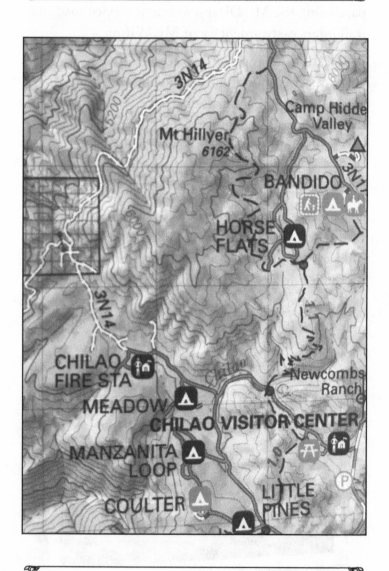

The map shows:
- 3N14
- Camp Hidde[n] Valley
- Mt Hillyer 6162
- BANDIDO
- HORSE FLATS
- CHILAO FIRE STA
- MEADOW
- CHILAO VISITOR CENTER
- Newcombs Ranch
- MANZANITA LOOP
- COULTER
- LITTLE PINES
- Chilao

MT. HILLYER

SILVER MOCCASIN, MT. HILLYER TRAILS

From Chilao to Mt. Hillyer is 6 miles round trip with 1,000-foot gain

Even on the Angeles National Forest map, the trail looks intriguing: a red dashed line zigzags through the heart of the San Gabriel Mountains and connects Chantry Flat and Shortcut Station, Chilao, Cloudburst and Cooper Canyon. Designed by the Los Angeles Area Council of the Boy Scouts of America, the 53-mile long Silver Moccasin Trail extends from Chantry Flat to the mountain named for the founder of the Boy Scouts, Lord Baden-Powell. Scouts who complete the weeklong trek earn the prized Silver Moccasin award.

One pretty stretch of the Silver Moccasin Trail tours the Chilao country, a region of giant boulders and gentle, Jeffrey pine-covered slopes. Happily, this slice of the San Gabriels escaped nearly unscathed from the 2009 Station Fire that burned so many slopes and canyons nearby.

Another path—Mt. Hillyer Trail—leads to the top of 6,162-foot Mt. Hillyer. From the top, you'll get views to the north of the desert side of the San Gabriels. As high country peaks go, Mt. Hillyer is an easy ascent. Quickest, but not the most scenic way to the top (a 2.6 mile round trip hike with a 600-foot gain) is from Horse Flats Campground.

During the early 1870s, stagecoach robber/horse and cattle thief Tiburcio Vasquez and his gang hid out in the Chilao country. The stolen horses were pastured in secluded grassland we now call Horse Flats. Vasquez, last of a generation of bandits to operate out of the Southern California backcountry, was captured in 1874.

Many reporters visited Vasquez in his Los Angeles jail cell, and the highwayman soon found himself quite a celebrity. He was not an ordinary criminal, he told the press, but a patriotic Californio whose goal was to rid Southern California of the gringo influence. Southern Californians loved Vasquez's stories and knew that in a small way he represented the end of an era; nevertheless, he was sent to the gallows in 1875.

DIRECTIONS: From the Foothill Freeway (210) in La Canada, exit on Angeles Crest Highway (2) and wind 27 miles up the mountain road to the signed turnoff for the Chilao Visitor Center. Turn left and follow the paved road past the (closed) visitor center 0.5 to signed Silver Moccasin Trail on your right and a small amount of parking.

THE HIKE: Switchbacks lead up chaparral slopes dotted with Jeffrey pine for a mile to top a minor ridge and reach a signed junction. Here you leave Silver Moccasin Trail (which swings southeast toward Angeles Crest Highway and Cooper Canyon and go right with a retiring dirt road 100 yards toward Horse Flats Campground where you meet and join signed Mt. Hillyer Trail.

The path switchbacks up pine-, incense cedar- and scrub oak-covered slopes. Some big boulders suggest a perfect hideout, whether you're fleeing the sheriff or the stresses of modern life.

Up top, the broad summit of Mt. Hillyer may remind you of what Gertrude Stein said of Oakland: "There's no there, there." The summit is not a commanding pinnacle, but a forested flat. With all those trees in the way, you'll have to walk a few hundred yards along the ridgeline to get your view of the green country to the south and the brown, wrinkled desert side of the San Gabriels to the north.

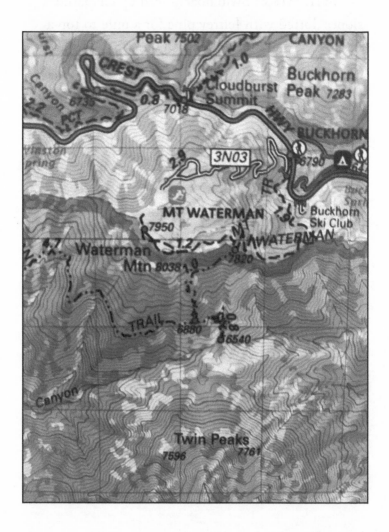

MT. WATERMAN

MT. WATERMAN, TWIN PEAKS TRAIL

To Mt. Waterman is 5.5 miles round trip with 1,300-foot elevation gain; to Twin Peaks is 9.5 miles round trip

Mt. Waterman is best known for its ski area, located just an hour or so drive from greater Los Angeles. Alpine scenery and a decent amount of "heaven sent" snowfall contribute to Waterman's popularity. Mt. Waterman lays claim to installing the first chairlift (1941) in California.

When Mt. Waterman is snow-less, the 8,038-foot peak becomes the province of hikers. Waterman's location adjoining the San Gabriel Wilderness means the mountain shares some of the remoteness of this rough-and-rugged country.

More remote than Mt. Waterman (and offering better clear-day views) is Twin Peaks. The boulder-strewn summits of 7,761-foot East Twin Peak and 7,596-foot West Twin Peak, as well as the ridgeline, offer commanding panoramas of the L.A. Basin, Palomar Mountain, Mt. San Jacinto, and Catalina Island.

The peak is named for Robert Waterman, mountain man and a ranger in the San Gabriel Forest Reserve, but it was *supposed* to be named for his wife Liz, who accompanied him on an epic 3-week hike across the range in 1889. Liz constructed a rock cairn on the summit and named it "Lady Waterman's Peak." Due to the male chauvinism of the time, "Lady" was left off the map and Liz never given credit, despite years of effort by Robert Waterman to restore the full name to the peak.

Mt. Waterman Trail ascends two miles through a peaceful forest of Jeffrey pine and incense cedar to a fork in the trail, where you can choose to climb Waterman, Twin Peaks, or both. You can reach the top of Waterman with modest effort, while hiking to the summit of East Twin Peak is a challenging down and up trek.

DIRECTIONS: From the Foothill Freeway (210) in La Canada, exit on Highway 2 and drive 33 miles. Half a mile past the Mt. Waterman ski lift, look right for road paddle 58/00, then park in the large lot on the left (north) side of the highway. (If you arrive at the entrance of Buckhorn Campground, you passed the trailhead.) Walk carefully along the south side of the highway to a dirt road with a yellow steel gate across it.

THE HIKE: Hike 100 yards or so up Mt. Waterman Road to meet Mt. Waterman Trail. Leave behind the sight and sounds of the highway as the trail ascends through mixed conifer forest. A mile out, reach a ridge extending east from the shoulder of Waterman, and continue the climb to a signed junction at the two-mile mark.

The left fork leads to Twin Peaks; turn right to continue your ascent of Waterman. About 0.1 mile short of the summit, the trail divides. To the left, a short steep path leads to the south end of the summit. Continue straight with Mt. Waterman Trail 0.25 to the center of the peak and trail's end at a junction with a dirt road (optional return route through the ski resort).

To Twin Peaks: From the junction, the slender trail descends past dispersed pines. Look up at Triplet Rocks, an aptly named formation on the eastern shoulder of Twin Peaks. Descend switchbacks to a junction with Three Points Trail, a mile from Mt. Waterman Trail. Then down another 0.75 mile to a saddle.

Now the fun begins: 1.25 miles with a 1,200-foot gain to the top of East Twin Peak. Hike on. No switchbacks. Just follow rock cairns on the extremely steep ascent. About 0.2 mile short of the summit, reach the ridge between East Twin Peak and West Twin Peak. The trail goes left to Twin Peaks East (though there is a trail-less route to West Twin Peak).

Continue your climb to the rocky summit. Lots of trees up here, so rather than one grand panorama, you'll get a series of tree-framed views. Wonderful, well worth the climb.

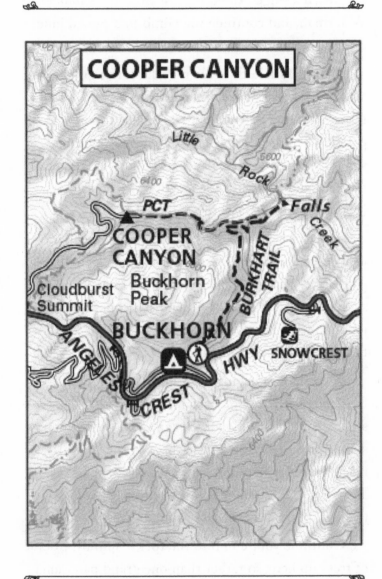

COOPER CANYON

Little
Rock
5600
6400
PCT
Falls
Creek
COOPER
CANYON
Buckhorn
Peak
Cloudburst
Summit
BURKHART TRAIL
BUCKHORN
SNOWCREST
ANGELES CREST HWY

TheTrailmaster.com

COOPER CANYON

BURKHARDT, PACIFIC CREST TRAILS

From Buckhorn Camp to Cooper Canyon Falls is 3 miles round trip with 800 foot elevation loss; to Cooper Canyon Trail Camp is 5 miles round trip

Apparently far more Southern Californians regard the Mt. Waterman area as a place to ski rather than hike. How else to explain why slopes that are so crowded in winter are empty in summer?

The deep woodsy canyons just north of Mt. Waterman and Kratka Ridge are a delight. Maybe travelers don't know about the impressive tall trees—forests of incense cedar, Jeffrey pine and sugar pine. And of course there's Cooper Canyon Falls, impressive in full spring vigor, and even delightful in summer spilling slowly and quietly into an alder-shaded pool.

In the late 19th and early 20th centuries, hunters nailed a pair of buck horns to a tree in order to mark one of their favorite encampments—Buckhorn Camp. Two of this hunting era's most avid hunters, brothers Ike and Tom Cooper from the city of San Gabriel, hunted deer and bear in a rugged canyon below Buckhorn Camp. The canyon soon became known as Cooper Canyon.

After 1915 (when the Forest Service banned most hunting in the San Gabriel Mountains), game trails became hiking trails and hunters' camps became public campgrounds. Buckhorn Campground is one of the most pleasant places to overnight in Angeles National Forest.

The family-friendly route to Cooper Canyon Falls begins on the Burkhardt Trail aka High Desert National Recreation, which traverses the Pleasant View Ridge Wilderness and extends to the Devil's Punchbowl on the desert side of the mountain range.

DIRECTIONS: From the Foothill Freeway (210) in La Canada, take Angeles Crest Highway (2) 34 miles to the signed turnoff for Buckhorn Campground. Turn left and follow the camp road a short mile to its end at the hikers' parking area.

THE HIKE: From the north end of the parking lot, join Burkhardt Trail as it heads north down-canyon above Buckhorn Creek. Happy campers enjoy the small waterfalls, cascades and swimming holes along the creek below the camp.

Are we hiking in the High Sierra? The towering, stately conifers with almost no undergrowth beneath them, the bold rock outcroppings, the steep canyon walls...the San Gabriels sure resemble the southern Sierra along this stretch of trail.

After a 1.25 mile descent, the path reaches the bottom of Cooper Canyon and turns east, arriving soon thereafter at a signed junction with Pacific Crest Trail. A left on the PCT leads 1.25 miles along the creek to Cooper Canyon Trail Camp and about 2,000 miles or so to Canada. A far more popular option is to bear right and proceed east 0.1 mile to Cooper Canyon Falls. Reach the falls by carefully descending a short, steep footpath down to the creek.

Wilderness well-named: Pleasant View Ridge

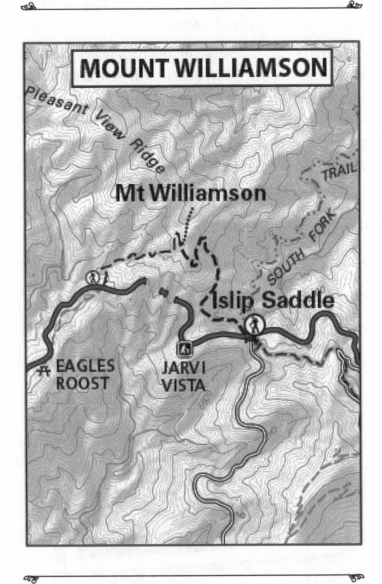

MOUNT WILLIAMSON

Pleasant View Ridge

Mt Williamson

TRAIL

SOUTH FORK

Islip Saddle

EAGLES ROOST

JARVI VISTA

MOUNT WILLIAMSON

PACIFIC CREST TRAIL

From Islip Saddle to Mt. Williamson is 5 miles round trip with 1,600-foot elevation gain

Mt. Williamson stands head and shoulders above other crests along Angeles Crest Highway. The 8,214-foot peak offers grand views of earthquake country—the Devil's Punchbowl, San Andreas Fault and the fractured northern edges of the San Gabriel Mountains.

Desert views this peak may offer, but Mt. Williamson is anything but a desert peak. It's plenty green and bristling with pine and fir.

The summit of Mt. Williamson is the high point and culmination of well-named Pleasant View Ridge, a chain of peaks that rises from the desert floor to Angeles Crest Highway. It's quite a contrast to stand atop the piney peak, which is snow-covered in winter, and look down upon Joshua trees and the vast sandscape of the Mojave Desert.

Pleasant View Ridge Wilderness, 26,757 acres located north of the Angeles Crest Highway where the San Gabriel Mountains slope north to meet the Mojave Desert, was designated in 2009.

Hot and cold, desert and alpine environments—these are the contrasts that make hiking in Southern California so very special.

Mountain namesake Major Robert Stockton Williamson first explored the desert side of the San Gabriels in 1853. Williamson, a U.S. Army mapmaker led an expedition in a successful search for a railroad route around or through the mountains. Williamson's report to Congress detailed two routes: Cajon Pass on the east end of the San Gabriels and Soledad Canyon on northwest.

Two fine segments of Pacific Crest Trail ascend Mt. Williamson from Angeles Crest Highway. One trail leads from Islip Saddle, the other from a saddle 1.5 miles farther west. With a car shuttle, you could hike both. However, don't even think about walking Angeles Crest Highway to make a loop trip; it's unsafe to walk the highway and through two tunnels en route.

DIRECTIONS: From the Foothill Freeway in La Canada, follow Angeles Crest Highway (2) 41 miles to the parking area at Islip Saddle on the left (north) side of the highway.

THE HIKE: At Islip Saddle, note South Fork Trail (descending northeast toward Devil's Punchbowl County Park.) From the north side of the parking lot, join signed Pacific Crest Trail as it ascends somewhat aggressively along the eastern shoulder of Mt. Williamson and through a forest of Jeffrey and ponderosa pine.

A bit more than 2 miles out, near 8,000 feet in elevation, reach a junction. PCT continues west. Take the fainter path north on a steep ascent passing scattered white fir. Enjoy over-the-shoulder views south into the heart of the rugged San Gabriel Wilderness. Keep hiking north on the trail, which gets increasingly sketchy as it passes over a few bumps and reaches the summit of Mt. Williamson.

Enjoy dramatic views of the desert. Gaze out at the many playas (dry lake beds), buttes and mountain ridges of the dry lands below. At the base of Mt. Williamson lies that greatest of earthquake faults—the San Andreas Rift Zone. Most striking of all is the view of Devil's Punchbowl and its jumbled sedimentary strata.

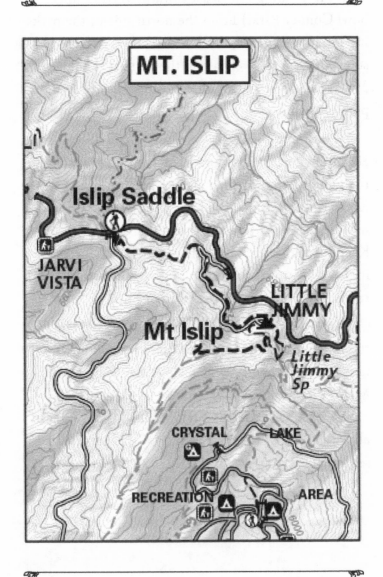

MT. ISLIP

Islip Saddle

JARVI VISTA

LITTLE JIMMY

Mt Islip

Little Jimmy Sp

CRYSTAL LAKE

RECREATION AREA

MT. ISLIP

MT. ISLIP TRAIL

From Angeles Crest Highway to Little Jimmy Trail Camp is 3 miles round trip with 500-foot elevation gain; to Mt. Islip is 5 miles round trip with 1,100-foot gain

Mt. Islip (pronounced eye-slip) is by no means one of the tallest San Gabriel mountain peaks, but its relatively isolated position on the spine of the range makes it stand out. The summit offers the hiker fine views of the middle portion of the Angeles National Forest high country and of the metropolis.

Mt. Islip has long been a popular destination for hikers. Occidental College students built a huge cairn (heap of boulders), dubbed "Occidental Monument," atop the summit in 1909. The monument, which had the name Occidental on top, stood about two decades, until the Forest Service cleared the summit to make room for a fire lookout tower. The monument and fire lookout are long gone, but the stone foundation of the fire lookout's living quarters still remains.

One early visitor to the slopes of Mt. Islip was popular newspaper cartoonist Jimmy Swinnerton (1875-1974), well known in the early years of the 20th century for his comic strip "Little Jimmy." By the time he was in his thirties, hard-working, hard-drinking Swinnerton was suffering from the effects of exhaustion, booze, and tuberculosis. His employer and benefactor, William Randolph Hearst, sent him to the desert to dry out, but Swinnerton opted for the mountains.

During the summers of 1908 and 1909 Swinnerton often set up camp near Gooseberry Spring, which soon became known as Little Jimmy Spring, and entertained passing hikers with sketches of his Little Jimmy character. His campsite now bears the name of Little Jimmy Trail Camp.

DIRECTIONS: From the Foothill Freeway (210) in La Canada, exit on Angeles Crest Highway (2) and proceed some 41 miles to signed Islip Saddle. On the north side of the highway, is a large parking area.

THE HIKE: The trail begins as a dirt road shaded by Jeffrey and sugar pine. A half-mile ascent leads to a three-way junction. To the right is the old crest trail coming up from Islip Saddle. The forest road continues to Little Jimmy Trail Camp.

Bear left on the signed trail to Little Jimmy. The trail stays just below and parallel to the road as it ascends a mile over forested slopes to Little Jimmy

Trail Camp. The camp, popular with youth groups, has tables, stoves and restrooms. A side trail leads 0.25 mile southeast to all-year Little Jimmy Spring.

At the west end of camp, join the signed trail to Mt. Islip. Ascend 0.5 mile of switchbacks through piney woods to a sharp ridgeline. From atop the ridge, enjoy great views of Crystal Lake, the San Gabriel Wilderness, and canyons cut by Bear Creek and the San Gabriel River.

The trail turns east and follows the ridge for another 0.5 mile to the 8,250-foot peak. Summit views include ski areas and Mt. Waterman to the west and Mt. Baden-Powell to the east.

Jimmy Swinnerton sketched some of his popular "Little Jimmy" comic strips in the San Gabriel Mountains, where he camped during the summers of 1908 and 1909.

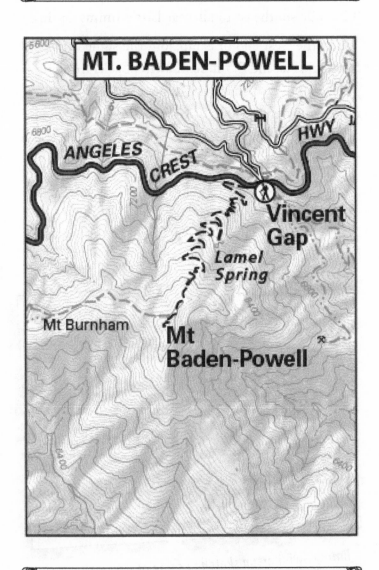

MT. BADEN-POWELL

MT. BADEN-POWELL

MT. BADEN-POWELL TRAIL

From Vincent Gap to summit is 8 miles round trip with 2,800-foot elevation gain

This trail and peak honor Lord Baden-Powell, a British Army officer who founded the Boy Scout movement in 1907. The well-engineered trail, grooved into the side of the mountain by the Civilian Conservation Corps in the mid-1930s, switchbacks up the northeast ridge to the peak.

The peak was once known as North Baldy, before Southern California Boy Scouts lobbied the Forest Service for a name change. Mt. Baden-Powell is the terminus of the scouts' 53-mile Silver Moccasin Trail, a rugged week-long backpack through the San Gabriels.

The trail follows a moderate, steady grade to the top of the mountain, where there's a monument honoring Powell. On the summit, you'll meet those ancient survivors, the limber pines, and be treated to superb views across the Mojave Desert and down into the Iron Fork of the San Gabriel River.

DIRECTIONS: Take the Angeles Crest Highway (2) for 53 miles from La Cañada to the Vincent Gap Parking Area. The signed trailhead is at the northwest edge of the parking area. If you're coming from the east, take Interstate 15 to the Wrightwood exit, three miles south of Cajon Pass. Proceed 8 miles west on Highway 138 to its intersection with Highway 2. Turn left on Highway 2 and drive 14 miles to the trailhead.

THE HIKE: Begin the ascent from Vincent Gulch Divide, a gap separating the upper tributaries of the San Gabriel River to the south from Big Rock Creek to the northwest. The trail switchbacks southwest through Jeffrey pine and fir. The trail numbers more than three dozen of these switchbacks; however, so many inspiring scenes compete for the hiker's attention it's hard to get an accurate count.

In 1.5 miles, a side trail (unmarked) leads a hundred yards to Lamel Spring, an inviting resting place and the only dependable water en route.

With increased elevation, the switchbacks grow shorter and steeper and the vegetation changes from fir to lodgepole pine. Soon, even the altitude-loving lodgepoles give way to the heartiest of pines, the limber pine. A half-mile from the summit, around 9,000 feet in elevation, the first of these squat, thick-trunked limber pines come into view.

To Limber Pine Forest: A tiny sign points right (southwest) to the limber pine stand, 0.125 mile. These wind-loving, subalpine dwellers are one of the few living things that can cope with the rarefied atmosphere. *Pinus flexilis*, botanists call the species, for its long, droopy, flexible branches. They bow and scrape like hyperextended dancers and appear to gather all their nourishment from the wind.

Back on the main trail, a few more switchbacks bring you atop the ridge where Mt. Baldy can be glimpsed. Walk along the barren crest and intersect the Pacific Crest Trail. PCT swoops off to Little Jimmy Spring.

Continue past the limber pines to the summit. A concrete monument pays homage to Lord Baden-Powell. Enjoy the superb view out across the Mojave to the southern Sierra and east to Baldy, San Gorgonio and San Jacinto.

The enduring statuesque limber pine, some 1,500 years old.

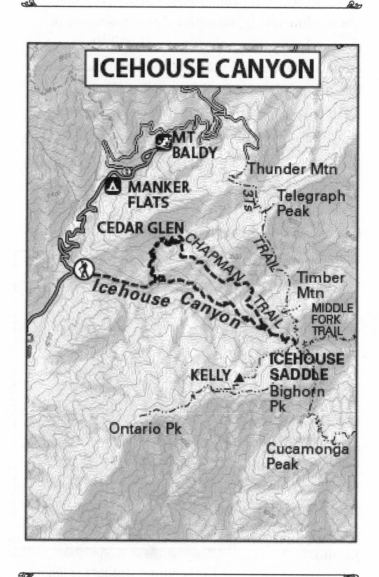

ICEHOUSE CANYON

MT BALDY

Thunder Mtn

MANKER FLATS

Telegraph Peak

CEDAR GLEN

CHAPMAN TRAIL

3TS TRAIL

Icehouse Canyon

Timber Mtn

MIDDLE FORK TRAIL

ICEHOUSE SADDLE

KELLY

Bighorn Pk

Ontario Pk

Cucamonga Peak

TheTrailmaster.com

ICEHOUSE CANYON

ICEHOUSE CANYON TRAIL

From Icehouse Canyon to Icehouse Saddle is 7 miles round trip with 2,600-foot gain

Icehouse Canyon Trail, leading from Icehouse Canyon to several 8,000-foot peaks, is an ideal introduction to the high-country delights of Cucamonga Wilderness. The precipitous subalpine slopes of the wilderness, thickly forested with sugar pine, ponderosa pine and incense cedar, offer fresh mountain air and a network of good footpaths.

The 12,781-acre wilderness includes the Three T's—Timber Mountain, Telegraph Peak and Thunder Mountain—as well as 8,859-foot Cucamonga Peak, easternmost sentinel of the San Gabriel Mountains.

Icehouse Canyon is the hiker's only easy entry into the Cucamonga high country. The saddle and nearby peaks offer fine views to the hiker. Peak-baggers like this trail because several peaks are within "bagging distance" of Icehouse Saddle.

Icehouse Canyon was long known as Cedar Canyon because, as the story goes, the great cedar beams for Mission San Gabriel were logged here. The name Icehouse originated in the 1860s when ice was cut in the lower canyon and shipped to San Gabriel Valley residents.

Well-constructed Chapman Trail, named for the family that built the Icehouse Canyon resort in the 1920s, heads up Cedar Canyon to Cedar Glen, climbs out of Cedar Canyon, then contours on a steady grade back over to Icehouse Canyon.

DIRECTIONS: From the Foothill Freeway (210) in Claremont, exit on Baseline Road and head west one block to Padua Avenue. Turn right and drive north 1.7 miles to a stop sign and an intersection with Mt. Baldy Road. Turn right and drive 7.2 miles to the Angeles National Forest's Mt. Baldy Visitor Center in Mt. Baldy Village. Proceed another 1.5 miles past the village to Icehouse Canyon parking area.

(In addition to displaying an Adventure Pass on your vehicle, you'll also need to obtain a wilderness permit from the Mt. Baldy Visitor Center.)

THE HIKE: The trail leads east along the floor of the canyon. The path stays close to the oak- and spruce-shaded creek and passes some cabins. After 1.5 miles, the trail forks. Take the "high route," the Chapman Trail, 1 mile to Cedar Flats and then 3 miles up to Icehouse Saddle, or continue straight ahead on the shorter and steeper Icehouse Canyon Trail directly up the canyon.

Icehouse Canyon Trail leads past more cabins and climbs up the north slope of the canyon, before dropping down again and crossing the creek. The trail switchbacks steeply through pine and spruce, which frame fine vistas of Old Baldy. Chapman Trail and Icehouse Canyon Trail intersect and a single trail ascends a steep 0.75 mile to the top of Icehouse Saddle.

Enjoy the view and return the same way, or choose among the fine trails that lead from Icehouse Saddle. You can continue eastward and drop down the Middle Fork Trail to Lytle Creek. A right (southeast) turn puts you on a trail that climbs two miles to Cucamonga Peak. A sharp right southwest leads 2.5 miles to Kelly's Camp and Ontario Peak. And a left on the Three T's Trail takes you past Timber Mountain, Telegraph Peak and Thunder Mountain, and then drops to Baldy Notch.

Hike into the Cucamonga Wilderness and into some curious mountain history.

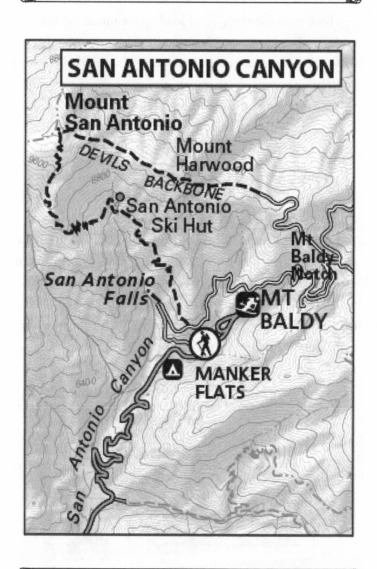

SAN ANTONIO CANYON

Mount San Antonio

Mount Harwood

DEVILS BACKBONE

San Antonio Ski Hut

San Antonio Falls

Mt Baldy Notch

MT BALDY

San Antonio Canyon

MANKER FLATS

SAN ANTONIO CANYON

SKI HUT TRAIL

To San Antonio Falls is 2.5 miles round trip with 200-foot elevation gain; to San Antonio Canyon Overlook is 6.5 miles round trip with 2,600-foot gain; to Mt. Baldy summit is 8.5 miles round trip with 3,800-foot gain

The attractive trail leading up San Antonio Canyon to the top of Baldy is a Trailmaster favorite. Hikers of all ages and abilities will enjoy the short excursion to three-tiered, 60-foot San Antonio Falls.

Two more destinations beckon: the Sierra Club ski hut, where there's a cool spring, and a high ridge overlooking San Antonio Canyon. Hikers in top form will relish the challenge of the climb to the top and summit views: a panorama of desert and ocean, the sprawling Southland and the southern High Sierra.

DIRECTIONS: From the Foothill Freeway (210) in Claremont, exit on Baseline Road and head west one block to Padua Avenue. Turn right and drive north 1.7 miles to a stop sign and an intersection with

Mt. Baldy Road. Turn right and drive 7.2 miles to the Angeles National Forest's Mt. Baldy Visitor Center in Mt. Baldy Village, then 4 more miles to Manker Flats Campground and almost to the end of the road. Look for Falls Road on the north side of the road. Park along Mt. Baldy Road and hike up Falls Road.

THE HIKE: Walk up the fire road (closed to public traffic). After modest ascent, behold San Antonio Falls. (You can descend to the base of the falls on rough trail.) Continue walking along the road (unpaved beyond the falls) and look sharply left for an unsigned trail.

The trail ascends very steeply along the side of San Antonio Canyon. Appreciate this steep path: it has a hand-hewn, unobtrusive look and follows the natural contours of the land. Jeffrey pine, ponderosa pine and fir shade the path.

From the ski lift road it's 1.75 miles by trail to Sierra Club ski hut. Near the hut, constructed in 1935, is a cool and refreshing spring. Just past the ski hut, the trail crosses a tiny creek, and snakes through a boulder field. Beyond the boulders the trail ascends via a 0.5-mile series of steep switchbacks to a ridge-top overlooking the headwaters of San Antonio Canyon. Enjoy great views from the tree-shaded ridgetop.

Peak-baggers will continue up the extremely rugged trail for another mile to the summit. The trail is rough and tentative in places, but rocks piled in cairns help you stay on course. Take in good views of Devil's Backbone, the sharp ridge that connects the east slope of Mt. Harwood with the top of the ski slope, coming up from Baldy Notch.

Atop Baldy's crown, rock windbreaks offer shelter. Enjoy vistas view of San Gabriel and San Bernardino mountain range peaks, the Mojave and the metropolis.

Return the same way or take Devil's Backbone Trail to Mt. Baldy Notch. From the Notch, follow the fire road down Manker Canyon back to the trailhead or ride down the ski lift.

Top of the San Gabriels, top of the world

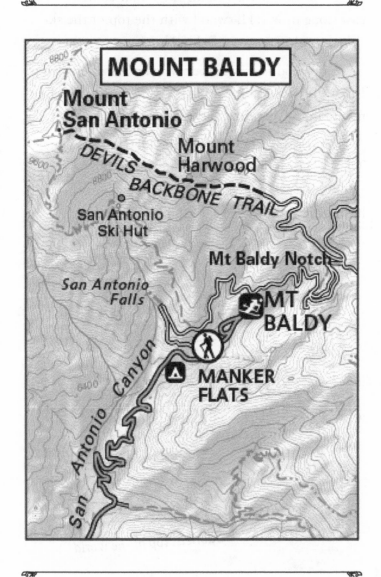

MOUNT BALDY

Mount San Antonio

Mount Harwood

DEVILS BACKBONE TRAIL

San Antonio Ski Hut

Mt Baldy Notch

San Antonio Falls

MT BALDY

San Antonio Canyon

MANKER FLATS

Mount Baldy

Devil's Backbone Trail

From Baldy Notch via ski lift, then to Mt. Baldy summit is 6.4 miles round trip with 2,200-foot gain; (without ski lift) 13 miles round trip with 3,800-foot gain

Mt. San Antonio, more commonly known as Mt. Baldy, is the highest peak (10,068 feet) in the mountains and visible from much of the Southland. Its summit gleams white in winter and early spring, gray in summer and fall. Old Baldy is so big and bare that it seems to be snow-covered even when it's not.

Baldy is a bit austere from afar, but up-close, the white granite shoulders of the mountain are softened by a forest of pine and fir. Padres of Mission San Gabriel, circa 1790, named the massive stone bulwark after Saint Anthony, a 13th-century friar from Padua, Italy. In the 1870s, gold-seekers dubbed the massive peak a more earthly "Old Baldy."

From Baldy Notch, Devil's Backbone Trail offers a moderately challenging route to the summit. This popular trail is the one most hikers associate with

Baldy. Clear-day views from the top offer a panorama of desert and ocean, the sprawling Southland and the Southern High Sierra.

Devil's Backbone Trail is one of the most memorable hiking experiences in Southern California. A narrow path crosses a narrow ridge with steep drop-offs to the north and south. (This is no place for those with a fear of heights or a place to hike in high winds or in winter conditions.)

An alternative is to walk up a fire road to Baldy Notch. This option adds 3 miles each way and a 1,300-foot gain to the hike. The fire road switchbacks up the west side of steep San Antonio Canyon, offers a good view of San Antonio Falls, then climbs northward to the top.

DIRECTIONS: From the Foothill Freeway (210) in Claremont, exit on Baseline Road and head west one block to Padua Avenue. Turn right and drive north 1.7 miles to a stop sign and an intersection with Mt. Baldy Road. Turn right and drive 7.2 miles to the national forest's Mt. Baldy Visitor Center in Mt. Baldy Village, then 4 more miles up to Manker Flats Campground. Park along Mt. Baldy Road and hike up Falls Road.

Those riding the ski lift will continue 0.25 mile past the campground to the Baldy Ski Lifts and free parking. Purchase a ticket and ride the ski lift up to Baldy Notch. (The lift is operated weekends and holidays all year.)

THE HIKE: From Baldy Notch, a wide gravel path leads to a commanding view of the desert. Join a chair lift access/fire road, and ascend a broad slope forested in Jeffrey pine and incense cedar. The road ends in about 1.25 miles at the top of a ski lift.

From here, a trail leads onto a sharp ridge, the Devil's Backbone. Look north down into the deep gorge of Lytle Creek, and south into San Antonio Canyon. Pass around the south side of Mt. Harwood, "Little Baldy," and up through scattered stands of lodgepole pine.

Reach a tempestuous saddle (Hold onto your hat!) and continue on a steep rock-strewn pathway that zigzags past wind-bowed limber pine to the summit. Atop Baldy's crown, rock windbreaks offer shelter. Enjoy vistas of San Gabriel and San Bernardino mountain peaks, the Mojave and the metropolis.

Devil's Backbone Trail, a narrow trail along a narrow ridge. What a hike!

JOHN MCKINNEY

John McKinney is the author of 30 hiking-themed books (narratives, guidebooks, and books for children), including *Hiking on the Edge: Dreams, Schemes, and 1600 Miles on the California Coastal Trail.*

HIKE Santa Barbara and *HIKE Griffith Park* are among the titles in the The Trailmaster's "Best Day Hikes" series, designed to give hikers the information they need in an engaging and easily accessible way.

For 18 years, he wrote a weekly hiking column for the *Los Angeles Times*, and has hiked and enthusiastically described more than ten thousand miles of trail across America and around the world. John, a.k.a. The Trailmaster, has written more than a thousand articles about hiking plus numerous trail guidebooks in his "Best Day Hikes" series, including regional bestsellers, *HIKE Southern California* and *Day Hiker's Guide to California's State Parks.*

A passionate advocate for hiking and our need to reconnect with nature, John McKinney shares his expertise on radio, TV, online, and as a public speaker.

JOHN MCKINNEY:
"EVERY TRAIL TELLS A STORY."

HIKE ON.

TheTrailmaster.com